Chris~~tians~~
in
Families

Genesis
and
Exodus

Christians in Families

Genesis and Exodus

Ross T. Bender

Foreword by Willard M. Swartley

HERALD PRESS
Scottdale, Pennsylvania
Kitchener, Ontario
1982

Library of Congress Cataloging in Publication Data

Bender, Ross Thomas, 1929-
   Christians in families.

   (The Conrad Grebel lectures; 1981)
   Includes bibliographical references.
   1. Marriage—Religious aspects—Addresses, essays,
lectures.   2. Family—Addresses, essays, lectures.
3. Family—Religious life—Addresses, essays, lectures.
4. Sex (Theology)—Addresses, essays, lectures.
I. Title.
BV835.B44   241'.63   82-6058
ISBN 0-8361-3301-3 (pbk.)   AACR2

Scripture quotations are from the Revised Standard Version
of the Bible, copyrighted 1946, 1952, © 1971, 1973.

CHRISTIANS IN FAMILIES: GENESIS AND EXODUS
Copyright © 1982 by Herald Press, Scottdale, Pa. 15683
   Published simultaneously in Canada by Herald Press,
   Kitchener, Ont. N2G 4M5
Library of Congress Catalog Card Number: 82-6058
International Standard Book Number: 0-8361-3301-3
Printed in the United States of America
Design by David Hiebert

82 83 84 85 86 87 10 9 8 7 6 5 4 3 2 1

To Ruth

Contents

Foreword

I am happy to commend for your reading this Conrad Grebel Lectureship by Professor Ross T. Bender, who through his leadership in Christian education, both in the classroom and as dean of the Associated Mennonite Biblical Seminaries for seventeen years, has thought much and read widely on the topic here titled, *Christians in Families: Genesis and Exodus.* During these years as dean, Bender gave leadership to various faculty endeavors to ascertain the nature and appropriate expression of theological education. This experience has provided perspective for Bender's work in this lectureship, apparent in such characteristics as identifying basic assumptions, contributing global perspectives, and proposing theological critique.

The unique strength of the book, in my judgment, is that it puts the present somewhat faddish American discussion of family life within the broader historical and global perspective and, at the same time, brings to bear upon the current discussion rich biblical and theological insights from the Judeo-Christian tradition. The themes of covenant, commitment, and kingdom mission for the family guide the discussion.

Competing models to this biblical and Christian vision of sexuality, marriage, and family life are everywhere present in contemporary culture. This contribution argues that these competing models are often influenced by individualism and self-realization, values which stand opposed to Christian faith and life. Further, the competing models are often found wanting at the bar of long-term viability, emotional stability, and social coherence.

We are living in a time when much literature is available on problem areas or new expressions of sexuality, marriage, and family life. This book speaks to the heart and foundation of the entire discussion. Although it may not answer all the questions the reader may be led to ask, no reader can afford to ignore the issues and answers which it addresses.

As Christians in both family and congregational settings take up this study, I anticipate renewed commitment to the ideals here set forth. Bender does not dogmatically prescribe; he invites those who will to follow and to experience the rewards of affirming and living out these models in human community.

Willard M. Swartley, Executive Secretary
Conrad Grebel Projects Committee

Author's Preface

The invitation to me by the Conrad Grebel Lectureship Committee of the Mennonite Board of Education to prepare and deliver a series of lectures on the Christian family was a welcome one. For two decades I have been reading, studying, and teaching in this area; more recently I have been engaged to a limited extent in marriage and family counseling. It was therefore with considerable enthusiasm that I accepted the assignment to arrange my thoughts and experiences in a systematic way in the form of the present lectures.

The setting in which I carried out my further reflections and actually put pen to paper was ideal. Ruth and I with our daughter Anne (joined for a few months by our daughter Deborah) spent a delightful year in Geneva, Switzerland, where I also served as research associate to the World Council of Churches Office of Family Education and sat in on a number of classes at the University of Geneva. Our telephone rarely rang and I had no evening committee meetings. From my study window in our apartment on the sixth floor, I could look down on the busy street below to observe the comings and goings of our Genevan neighbors. From the balcony I could see the snowcapped Jura mountains just across the French border. On a clear day, Mont Blanc was visible from the corner where we caught the bus which took us to the airport or the university. For recreation we could walk in one of Geneva's many beautiful parks or catch the boat to Montreux and the Castle Chillon.

Though I had many things I wanted to say in these lectures, it was only after some months of catching up on the most recent literature that the organization of my lectureship began to take shape. Gradually there formed in my mind the awareness that the sexual revolution of which we are hearing so much is affecting how we live together as men and women in at least three distinctive ways. While the various groups or movements advocating change are not necessarily linked organizationally nor of one mind with respect to their goals or emphases, there is nonetheless a shared philosophical orientation among them. This is indicated by the social analysis which sees the problem to be addressed as one of oppression. Society, it is alleged, is made up of the oppressor and the oppressed. The oppressor is variously identified as the patriarchal family, traditional male/female roles, stereotyped gender definitions, social conventions and institutions governing sexual relations and marital patterns, and the bearing and rearing of children. Sometimes the oppressor or the enemy is identified as structures, traditions, or institutions; sometimes the oppressor is identified as males. The values stressed in the process of change, known as liberation, are individualism and self-realization.

Three major areas emerged in my thinking which gave shape and focus to the first three chapters. The first is the Christian response to the sexual revolution in terms of changing patterns in male/female gender role/identity and the partnership in life of women and men. In the past decade there has been a great deal of research into the biological, psychological, and sociological sources of maleness/femaleness and femininity/masculinity. As I reviewed some of this research and attempted to state some biblical perspectives on the issues being debated, I inquired not only into what it is that we are to be "liberated" *from* but also what we are being "liberated" *to* in the new social order which the sexual revolutionaries are preparing for us. This is the approach in each of the succeeding chapters as we examine critically the assumptions underlying various aspects of the liberation philosophy of the sexual revolution.

The second area focuses on the matter of how women and men live together in terms of intimate sexual union. This second aspect of the revolution, "liberation" from traditional patterns of sexual morality, is based on a sharp critique of the institution of monogamous marriage. Various forms of alternative intimate lifestyles are both described and advocated in a growing body of literature on the subject. We examine the subject of marriage from the biblical teaching on covenant and note how its assumptions differ from those of the proposed alternatives. In covenant marriage, the person seeks not first of all his/her own good but that of the covenant partner.

The progression of thought moves from a theology of sexuality through a theology of marriage to a theology of the family. The issue of having and raising children is yet a third area of the sexual revolution and underlies the current debate in all areas, not only contraception and abortion. I array myself neither with the absolutism of Pope John Paul II nor with the absolutism of Shulasmith Firestone *(The Dialectic of Sex)*, who is convinced that women will only be able to enter the labor force unconditionally like men do (and thus gain their full freedom and equality with men) when the "tyranny of the biological family" has been broken. In other words, since bearing and rearing children interfere with the sexual revolution, other ways will have to be found to perpetuate the species, assuming that that is still a worthwhile thing to do. I do take the position that our technology has once again outstripped our wisdom and that we have yet to comprehend the fuller implications for our sexuality when we separate intercourse from procreation. My favorite topic, however, has to do not primarily with whether we bring children into this world but what we do with them once they get here. I have included an intriguing idea which I have come across in several sources about the similarity between learning a language and learning gender/identity roles. The concept of learning a language is also a basic paradigm for the Christian nurture of children in the family.

In the first three chapters we look at the theme of "libera tion" as set forth by the advocates of the sexual revolution with respect to three aspects of sexuality, marriage, and the family: (a) "liberation" from gender role/identity stereotypes; (b) "liberation" from the confines of monogamous marriage; and (c) "liberation" from the "tyranny of the biological family," i.e., from bearing and rearing children. *Genesis* (in the title) refers to the origins of the family in the intention and initiative of God, who created persons in his own image as male and female. This is foundational not only for marital and family relationships but for all human relationships. *Exodus* refers to the liberation motif, a central theme of the sexual revolution which is strongly committed to freeing society from the "oppressor." It is not the exclusive property of the sexual revolutionaries, however, and may also stand for the biblical vision of liberation and freedom which we have attempted to articulate in these pages.

In the fourth chapter, the angle of vision shifts with regard to liberation of the family from destructive social and ideological forces which are shaping the family into their various molds. Up to this point we have viewed the family as the object of a variety of forces operating upon it. From this point on we view the family as subject, drawing on its resources to confront and challenge those forces and to create an environment in which its self-chosen values and goals are dominant. This chapter draws upon my research with a project of the WCC Office of Family Education, National Case Studies of the Family Unit in Changing Societies, popularly known as Family Power for Social Change.

Finally, based on the assumption that families of Christians are active subjects, not passive objects in society, we inquire into the nature of the mission God has entrusted to them. That mission is primarily to be a little community in which the love of the covenanting God is incarnated in human relationships. It is a community built on covenant in which love and fidelity are first principles. It is also a community which reaches out to share its resources with persons and families with whom it comes into contact. It is a community with a truly radical "alternative intimate lifestyle" in which authentic sexual liberation according to God's design is lived out. It is a place where the deepest intimacy needs of each member may be met and where persons are trained for human relationships and set free to give themselves to others as Christ gave himself.

The sexual revolution is placing a number of additional burning issues on the agenda of churches and families, including divorce and remarriage, abortion, and homosexuality. I have not dealt directly with these complex issues in this book, recognizing that each of them calls for a study in itself. I have participated in such studies conducted by the College Mennonite Church, Goshen, Indiana, of which I am a member (divorce and remarriage) and by the Mennonite Medical Association, which invited me to present papers at their symposia on abortion and homosexuality. Though each of the various aspects of the sexual revolution has its own distinctive character, it has become increasingly apparent to me that common to all of them are the underlying values of individualism and self-realization. We examine these assumptions in the light of the teaching and example of Christ, who laid down his life for his friends.

I am indebted to many persons who made this book possible: to the Conrad Grebel Lectureship Committee of the Mennonite Board of Education, especially its executive secretary, Willard Swartley, who provided counsel and encouragement; to their editorial advisory committee, John Lederach, Margaret Foth, and David Augsburger, who read the manuscript and gave constructive suggestions for improving it; to the administration of the Associated Mennonite Biblical Seminaries, who granted and supported my sabbatical leave;

to the Association of Theological Schools, which awarded me a faculty research grant; to Masamba ma Mpolo, executive director of the WCC Office of Family Education, who generously gave his permission to draw freely on the research findings of the Family Power for Social Change Project (see chapter 4); to the persons on various college and seminary campuses who sat patiently through my lectures and then made their comments and raised their questions which stimulated further thinking in my mind; to Jean Kelly and Frieda Claassen, who typed the final copy of the manuscript.

My greatest debt is, however, owed to my children, who have taught me the meaning of becoming a parent, and to my wife, Ruth, who not only typed the original manuscript but, what is more important, taught me the meaning of marriage through sharing her life and her love with me.

Ross T. Bender
Elkhart, Indiana
July 30, 1981

Christians in Families

Genesis
and
Exodus

1
And God Made Man and Woman: On the Community of Women and Men

"So God created man
in his own image,
in the image of God
he created him;
male and female he created them."
Genesis 1:27.

These simple words introduce us to a fascinating drama, a drama whose climax and denouement are still before us. It is not yet clear how the plot will be resolved on the human stage. In the scene we are witnessing today, the intensity of the action and the complexity of the plot increase. In this drama we are all actors; none is a spectator though we sometimes speak that way.

We are living in the midst of a sexual revolution, a time when all values regarding the way women and men live together are being reassessed. There is, in truth, literally no convention or conviction concerning sexuality, marriage, and the family that is not today being systematically challenged. Vance Packard stated in his book *The Sexual Wilderness* that "what in fact is occurring seems too chaotic and varied to describe yet as a revolution. A revolution implies a clear movement in an understood and generally supported direction." He expressed concern about the "normlessness which makes the contemporary problem a historically significant one."[1]

Since Packard wrote his book over a decade ago, there has been a veritable explosion of research and writing on this theme. The outline and direction of the revolution are becoming clearer. The word "liberation" is a key word in understanding what this revolution is all about. It is alleged that since time immemorial men have been oppressing women and that the values, conventions, institutions, and structures which have shaped the way that women and men live together as sexual beings are male centered; they give all the advantages to slightly less than half the human race.

The history of relationships between women and men, so filled with potential for creativity and growth for both, has been troubled from the very outset. The first transaction between Adam and Eve recorded in Scripture was an omen of the conflicts ahead. Adam blamed Eve for the trouble they got into and there has been controversy over the incident ever since. Some interpreters have said that the serpent approached Eve first because she was more gullible than Adam. That is why men have to be in charge of making the decisions and women are to be subordinate in all things. Other interpreters more recently have said that it was really the other way round. The serpent perceived that Eve was more intellectually curious than Adam; if it could seduce the theologically oriented Eve with the persuasive argument that "when you eat of it [i.e., the fruit] your eyes will be opened, and you will be like God, knowing good and evil," she in turn would seduce the more appetite-oriented Adam, who would be a pushover.

From Adam's initial attempt to blame Eve for his predicament on down through the history of civilization, the acrimony and alienation between men and women have increased. To their credit, most feminists in our time are subdued in their attacks on men in comparison with the innuendos and outright slurs of many of the highly respected fathers of the church. Tertullian's statement about women is an example. "You are the devil's gateway ... how easily you destroyed man, the image of God. Because of the death which you brought upon us, even the Son of God had to die."[2] In spite of his positive affirmation of marriage, Martin Luther had deeply ambivalent feelings about women in general and made some rather earthy statements about them. He saw their role in life as revolving around the three K's: *Kinder, Küche, and Kirche* (children, kitchen, and church).[3]

What shall we say about the seemingly innocent but allegedly devastating institutions like monogamous marriage and patriarchal families of which we are, for the most part, the products? Are they indeed as evil, monstrous, and destructive as their worst critics say they are? Do the sex roles traditionally associated with them put women down and keep them from becoming all that they might otherwise be? Are they artificially created and insensitively imposed by a male-oriented society and theologically supported by a conservative religious tradition? What, if anything, is natural or, if you wish, divinely ordained about them? These are indeed serious and far-reaching questions and they can no longer be ignored or flippantly brushed aside.

In considering these issues, we do well to ask respectfully what the advocates of the sexual revolution see as its goal and to inquire into the assumptions and values upon which their social vision is based. This is not a time for defensiveness but a time for serious confrontation. The Christian community must be candid in responding to the critique of its social vision in all areas affecting male-female relationships. Christians must be equally forthright in confronting the proponents of a new style of life about precisely where they intend to lead us and why.

Since the sex role system is at the heart of the issue being debated, the decade of the seventies has seen an intense investment of energy in researching the assumptions on which it is based. Is it rooted in the will of God? Is it fundamental for an orderly civilization? Will it bring social chaos if we tamper with it? Is it rooted in biology? Biologists, psychologists, sociologists, anthropologists, psychiatrists, and theologians have all contributed to the enormous mass of data which has been gathered.

Most sexual revolutionaries are not preoccupied with questions concerning the will of God. Nor are they inhibited by questions of social stability if that means preserving the status quo. They hold that the existing social order is demeaning and destructive and in any case is falling apart of its own accord out of its inherent deficiencies. That leaves the question of biology, and this is just where much of the research has focused.

Sex, Gender Identity, and Gender Role

One of the first questions asked by the mother and father of a new baby is, "Is it a girl or a boy?" The doctor takes a look at the genitals, and if nature has done a good job the answer is unequivocal. This, however, answers only the question of whether the infant is male or female. A more difficult question to answer at that point than the question of *sex* is the question of *gender.* Will the female child grow up to be *feminine?* Will the male child grow up to be *masculine?* And in the determination of these questions, nature counts on a heavy helping hand from nurture. In other words, *gender identity* is to a large extent (though not exclusively) dependent on the socialization process. That process begins with the first responses made by parents to the news of the baby's sex; it is as subtle as the different ways they hold girl babies and boy babies and as obvious as the different ways they decorate and furnish their rooms.

In 1966 the first Gender Identity Clinic was set up at Johns Hopkins Hospital in Baltimore.[4] It supplements the services of the hospital's Psychohormonal Research Unit. In addition to providing therapy for persons with defective sexual organs and psychosexual disorders, it conducts research into the origins of gender identity formation and malformation. An example would be transsexualism in which a person with a male body has a feminine gender identity (or vice versa). Is this incongruity nature's fault, i.e., a mix-up in the chromosomes and hormones? Or is it nurture's fault, i.e., did the parents and others send the growing child mixed messages? Such research provides insight into the origins of gender identity.

Gender identity is defined as "the sameness, unity and persistence of one's individuality as male, female, or ambivalent in greater or lesser degree, especially as it is experienced in self-awareness of gender roles."[5] Gender identity is the private, interior awareness of gender role. *Gender role* includes "everything that a person says or does to indicate to others or to the self the degree that one is either male, female, or ambivalent; it includes but is not restricted to sexual arousal and response; gender role is the public expression of gender identity."[5] In other words, they are two sides of the same coin, the private and the public. My gender identity is how I think of and experience my masculinity; my gender role is how I express it in ways you can observe. The term gender identity/role expresses the fact that they belong together.

The report on the Johns Hopkins gender research speaks of the psychosexual developmental process as a "sexual differentiation road map."[6] Nature's contribution is to start each one of us out on that journey down the road but there are many places where the road forks. The Johns Hopkins view is that biology does not absolutely determine which direction is taken at each fork though there is a predisposition. However, once a direction is taken and you pass through the gates leading in the male or female direction, the anatomical gates are locked behind you. However, in the human species, the sexual behavior gates have a measure of independence from the anatomical gates. In other words, for human beings sexual behavior is learned as well as built into the system. This is why nurture is so important in helping the growing child gain a sense of gender identity.[7]

In tracing the sexual differentiation route on the road map, let us begin at the very beginning, the fertilization of the egg. The embryo has the capacity to become either female or male; the growth buds of both organs are present. The gonads can develop into testicles or ovaries; the genital ducts or tubes can develop into the seminal vesicles, prostate gland, and vasa deferentia of a male, or the uterus, fallopian tubes, and upper vagina of a female. Similarly the little bud called a genital tubercule eventually becomes either a penis or a clitoris. During the first six weeks, the female embryo and the male embryo travel together down the same road until they come to the first fork of sexual differentiation. In more technical language, the embryo remains sexually undifferentiated for the first six weeks; it has the potential for going in either direction depending on its preprogrammed instructions.

It is significant to notice that these developing embryos each have 23 pairs of chromosomes and that each chromosome has hundreds of genes which determine such things as color of hair and eyes. Forty-five of the forty-six are X chromosomes; only one, the Y chromosome in the chromosomally male embryo, is distinctive. That's not a lot of difference on which to build a whole civilization and a myriad of stereotypes. From a chromosomal and genetic point of view, males and females are overwhelmingly more similar than they are different.

Another interesting thing to notice is what Money and Tucker call the Adam principle and the Eve basic model. Nature apparently prefers Eve as the basic model. If the embryo is left alone, it will naturally move in the female direction. "It takes a push at critical periods to make an individual, male or female, develop in the male direction; whenever the push is lacking or weak, the female pattern establishes itself."[8] That first push comes at six weeks when the Y chromosome gives instructions to the gonads (even the researchers don't know why or how) to become testicles.

The next push in the development of the male

embryo comes when the testicles begin manufacturing hormones, predominantly androgen, the masculinizing hormone, and secondarily estrogen, the feminizing hormone; both androgen and estrogen are produced by the testicles but not in equal amounts. The ovaries of the chromosomally female embryo produce a mixture of estrogen and androgen with the mix predominantly estrogen in this case. Both sexes produce both hormones as well as a third one, progestin, the pregnancy hormone. The critical variable is the mixture. In males, there is a greater proportion of androgen and in females of estrogen. The proportion varies from one individual to another; it also fluctuates within any given individual in the course of a lifetime. There is in each of us both masculine and feminine characteristics though masculine characteristics tend to be dominant in most males and feminine ones in most females.

At the time of the second critical push, the androgen produced in the male embryo prevents its female apparatus known as the müllerian structures from developing further. In the case of the female embryo, the male apparatus simply withers away without any interference from the female hormonal mix. It is this which has given rise to the Eve basic model and the Adam principle theories. It takes a special hormonal effort on the part of the body to become male and masculine; without it the embryo would develop normally into a female body. Nature's first choice is to make Eve. Perhaps that is why society has put so much energy into the masculine principle; nature needs all the help it can get from nurture to make a man!

The evidence of male vulnerability being greater than that of females (in spite of the risks of giving birth which males do not share) gives the lie to the stereotype that women are the weaker sex. Males are subject to a greater number and incidence of disorders passed on by the genes. The male fetus is less likely to survive in the womb until full term. To get a roughly equal number of boy babies and girl babies ending up at the finish line, the starter of the nine-month race must send off 140 males to 100 females; only 105 make it to the end, i.e., live birth. Even then males are more susceptible to disease than females from infancy on. At the end of the next race, from birth to death, again more females than males make it all or most of the way around the track; that is to say, the life expectancy of males is shorter than that of females.

In psychosexual development as well there is a greater vulnerability on the part of males. Money and Ehrhardt report that "there is a widespread convergence of data to support an estimated ratio of three or four obligative homosexual males to one such female. The disparity may be even greater."[9] That is, males have a greater tendency than females do to become homosexual in orientation. Or to put it another way, males have greater difficulty in establishing their gender/role identity than do females. Money and Ehrhardt also report that there is a higher proportion of male transsexuals seeking "hormonal and surgical sex reassignment."[9] These are only two different types of situations in which there are incongruities between gender identity (inner awareness) and gender role (outer expression) which create severe internal stress for such persons.

The Johns Hopkins researchers have concluded that so far as biology is concerned, the only irreducible differences between males and females have to do with their reproductive systems. The way they put it is that "men impregnate, women menstruate, gestate and lactate."[10] All else is subject to human intervention and manipulation through the socialization process, the injection of hormones, and surgery. There is, however, one limitation; once the nuclear core of a person's gender schema has been established as an adult, it cannot be changed.

There is evidence that boys can be raised as girls and vice versa, although the younger they are when gender is reassigned, the easier the process. There is also evidence that adult persons whose gender identity is ambivalent can have their gender reassigned (assisted by hormonal injections and surgery) in an attempt to bring their gender identity and gender role into internal and external harmony. It is only adults whose gender identity is confirmed who are unable to change. Of course, they are also highly unlikely to want to change.

Is the whole gender identity/role system, therefore, totally artificial, that is, altogether the result of human engineering? Would society be able to redesign its expectations and institutions and rid itself of all the existing stereotypes if there were a new social consensus on what is masculine and what is feminine? Some seem to think so, which is why they are pushing so hard for a revolution. The massive research into gender identity/ role which has recently been conducted by biologists and social scientists has had as its driving force the conviction that it is high time for change. What have they found?

First, many of the stereotypes, particularly the negative ones, are without foundation in fact. We need hardly be told who is supposed to be strong and who is thought to be weak by both women and men. We have already seen that that stereotype is mistaken. Furthermore it is a mistake for males and females to talk about each other as the "opposite sex." Professor Janet Saltzman Chafetz of the University of Houston asserts that "recent research clearly demonstrates that the stereotyped approach, which conceptualizes masculinity and femininity as opposite poles, is simple-minded and inaccurate as a description of real people."[11] The true picture is that it is possible for any given person to be either high or low on both masculine and feminine characteristics as measured by a variety of inventories or to have a mixture of such traits.

There are, of course, some categorical differences between the sexes, for example, skeletal structures and body builds. However, it does not follow that all males have larger bones and muscles than all females. We have already noted that we can say of a female that she is more likely to live to be 65 years of age or older than a male is. We cannot, of course, say of a particular couple that the wife will outlive her husband or that a brother will die before his sister if they are twins. Is the difference in life expectancy based on the added hazards faced by the man who is expected to go out into the stress of the workaday world and compete there in order to support his family? If so, in the new social order where his wife and his sister join him out there, we might expect them to sustain those same hazards with a consequent leveling out of male/female life spans. There is, however, some evidence that the discrepancy is not only environmental but biological in origin. Women consistently do better in stress tests than men.[12] Perhaps nature has equipped them in this way in order to sustain the stresses of pregnancy and childbirth.

Another consistent categorical difference is that males tend to be more aggressive in behavior than females from little on up. Professor Shirley Weitz of the New School for Social Research states that "clearly the personality attributes most closely allied with aggression such as dominance, independence and activity seem to have connotations of masculinity while their counterparts on the non-aggressive side, submission, dependence and passivity, arouse ideas of femininity."[13]

She warns the reader, however, to be careful not to assume that these characteristics describe every boy and every girl, every man and every woman. She also notes that the socialization process is a powerfully shaping influence in the way that males and females learn how to express aggressiveness.

Socialization, however, does not tell us all there is to know about this difference. There is clinical evidence to demonstrate that there are hormonal sources of this aggressiveness; in other words, there is a direct causal sequence between the presence of androgen and aggressive behavior. Very early in its development the initial spurt of androgen causes the embryo to differentiate into the male direction and the female (müllerian) structures to atrophy. The converse, however, does not follow in parallel fashion. The estrogen in the female embryo does not cause the male (wolffian) structures to atrophy; they simply wither away on their own unless androgen causes them to develop.[14]

Shall we therefore conclude that since androgen dominates estrogen to produce a male it is only natural that Andrew should dominate Esther? Does this greater male aggressiveness rooted in nature and encouraged by nurture tell us something profound about how society should go about the socialization process and build its institutions? Probably not! All we can safely conclude is that greater male aggressiveness, if it is undisciplined and unchanneled, leads to greater aggressive behavior. It is probably no coincidence that it is primarily males who engage in daredevil stunts, commit violent crimes, and fight wars. In and of itself, greater aggressiveness does not make males the natural unquestioned leaders of every human enterprise. What the socialization process can do and must do is to civilize aggressiveness and harness it for the larger social good. As Weitz puts it, "Even though the link between androgen and aggression is reasonably well established, no one would argue that men are totally at the mercy of their hormones, or that all must act in the same way given the similarities in their hormonal inputs."[15] Similarly, it cannot be argued that women are totally at the mercy of their hormones and that the menstrual cycle necessarily disqualifies them from certain parts of the world of work and public policy, as some would have it.

Revolution or Reform?

It is at this point that we may appropriately inquire into the social vision and its underlying value structure of those who propose basic changes in the gender identity/role system. Professor Shirley Weitz opens her recent book *Sex Roles* with a quotation from William L. O'Neill. "The lesson of history so far is that women cannot gain equality regardless of the methods used to obtain it." Professor Weitz continues:

> Or to put it more generally, the lesson of history is that women's roles do not change, and neither do men's. Except for a few technological innovations, women and men are performing just about the same functions within the family and society as they were in the middle ages or in prehistory, for that matter. The continuity extends across space as well as time.[16]

Women's roles, then and now, she says, revolve basically around the private sphere, child care, and household chores; men's roles involve the management of the public spheres of life, that is, economics and politics. The reference to space is based on her analysis of Russian, Eastern European, Swedish, Chinese, and Israeli societies in which "programs of sex role change have been based on the socialist dictum that only female participation in the labor force will lead to equality between the sexes."[17] In a word, her conclusion is that it hasn't. The much heralded changes toward equality in socialist societies have not materialized.

Following an excellent summary of the modern feminist movement in America, Weitz characterizes it as ideologically focused around two points of view, the reformist and the revolutionary. The reformists do not see man as the enemy but as fellow sufferer equally in need of liberation. Their common task is to humanize the present social situation, redistribute the traditional division of labor, and modify the rigid roles and expectations which weigh heavily and inflexibly on both women and men. The revolutionaries, on the other hand,

> offer a much more devastating critique of the sex role system, and, usually, of the accompanying societal structure as well. Many of the proponents of this view support the Marxist analysis of society and its consequences for the sex role system. They often speak of women explicitly as an oppressed class, and identify men and the patriarchal family system as the oppressors.[18]

Weitz indicates that "the ultimate aim of the revolutionary movement is the overthrow of the sex role system itself"[19] and quotes one such proponent who speaks of breaking "the tyranny of the biological family"[20] by providing for at least the option of artificial reproduction of children. In this way, women would be liberated from their labor pains and would be set free for the joys of labor, that is, for full participation in the world of work. The underlying assumption is that a woman's worth is based on her productivity in the public sphere and not in the private sphere of the home and family. To set women free for full participation in the public sphere, the mother-child bond will have to be effectively diminished and alternative child care arrangements will have to be set up. Only then will childbearing and childrearing no longer be the impediments to a woman's career and to her full participation in public affairs that they now are.

The revolutionary vision is radical because it goes beyond the sociological and psychological sources of the gender role system to the biological roots of that system in the reproductive process. It correctly sees that the only way to do away with that system is to substitute other means for reproduction and nurture of children.

Within the reformist school, there are a variety of positions. One is the androgynous view, a position adopted by Chafetz. She distinguishes this view from two others in terms of its ordering principle, "women and men are equal to each other." The women's liberationist ideology, she says, is "women over against men or separate from men." The feminist principle is "women are equal to men." Each ideology has its enemy, its analysis of the problem, its techniques for change, and its social vision of the goal for change. For androgynists and feminists the enemy is not men and the existing family structure as it is for the liberationists; rather it is cultural values and social institutions which are in need of correction. It is men and women working together who will bring about the needed modifications which will bring in the new social order. For androgynists, the key word to characterize the new order is *pluralism* (diversity within unity); for the feminists the key word is *integration* and for the liberationists it is *segregation.* The feminists are characterized as those who accept the masculine idiom as the measure of all good things and wish only to join that system, not restructure it. The liberationists reject the masculine order of things as oppressive to women and seek to replace it with a new social order determined by women.[21]

Whether or not these are the correct labels for these three points of view is not the basic issue. No doubt many feminists and women's liberationists would reject them as unfairly describing their movements. What Chafetz, following Gayle Yates, has described as the women's liberation movement, Weitz has characterized as the revolutionary position. What is helpful about this analysis is the distinctive character of various approaches to the issues; those advocating change in the gender role system are not a monolithic force operating on the same set of assumptions toward a common goal.

The androgynous ideal does not deny that there are differences between males and females, but it chooses to emphasize what they share in common, their human or personal qualities, aspirations, and ideals. Traditional sex roles are seen by androgynists to be decreasingly significant as tasks are shared in flexible ways by women and men. The ideal in both the domestic and public spheres would be for the "gender role stereotypes and sexual caste system"[22] to disappear altogether.

While the position advocated by Money and Tucker has much in common with the androgynous one, it differs in its insistence that the biological roots of maleness and femaleness do in fact make a significant difference in terms of masculinity and femininity. They hold that "the challenge is to reaffirm the genital and reproductive differences between the sexes as the foundation of the gender stereotypes."[23] The "nuclear core" of the gender schema must be safeguarded, in their view. However, the sex distinctions which have become "straitjackets" can safely be discarded. In between are a wide range of schema which are flexible and may be molded in many different ways. "Far from blurring difference between the sexes, freeing ourselves from stale, repetitive, artificially imposed patterns of difference will allow the real differences to emerge."[24] In working out the new schema, their emphasis is upon complementation and mutual enhancement.

Weitz sees gender roles as an interconnected system in which neither male nor female roles can be understood or modified without reference to the other. Therefore, for example, activity and passivity both are relative terms which are defined in relation to one another. They are psychological abstractions given their particular meanings in a social context. There are a whole host of such characteristics which belong together which a given society uses to describe masculinity and/or femininity. These vary from one society to another and from one generation to another.

Society also sets into motion the socialization process which builds these personality characteristics into the gender role and identity of its males and females. Some may have as their basis the physiological differences of the male/female reproductive system and the masculinizing/feminizing tendencies of the sex hormones. Still others are reflections of the collective social experience of the sexes in relationship down through the years as they have worked out a division of labor (e.g., men hunt food, women prepare it). This is what has brought about the predominantly male leadership in the public sphere and the predominantly female involvement in the private or domestic sphere. Still others are embedded in the value system of the community which may or may not be able to identify the source of these values but simply takes them for granted because they have been around for a long time.

The gender schema, however, are not simply abstract ideas but have been internalized into unconscious body movements, gestures, and emotional responses. Both the identified schema (male or female) and their complementary ones (female or male) have become part of the total inner apparatus of the personality; they are reinforced by the values of the person and of the society. That is why an attack on the existing gender roles is so massively resisted; it is experienced as an attack on the person himself/herself and on the conscious and unconscious foundations of the social order.

Some social scientists have come to conclude that at

the heart of the masculine/feminine system are two fundamentally complementary qualities, the *communal* and the *agentic.* Professors Janet T. Spence and Robert L. Helmreich of the University of Texas at Austin state, for example, "The core properties of femininity, we propose, can be usefully labeled or conceptualized as a sense of communion and the core properties of masculinity as a sense of agency."[25] They are, however, quite clear and emphatic that these are not mutually exclusive qualities; they may be found both in women and in men in a variety of mixtures. They also note that "some individuals may become truly androgynous in the sense of accepting equally their expressive and instrumental qualities and associating both with 'personhood' rather than with gender." They see such persons as the exception rather than the rule "even among those at higher levels of ego maturity."[26]

In discussing the complementarity of agency and communion, Spence and Helmreich assert that either property without the other can become destructive both to the individual and to society. Functioning in creative tension, within persons and between persons, they enhance both social and personal well-being. It is when agency or instrumentality function in isolation from the communal and the expressive that they go to seed. This is what gives rise to the negative masculine stereotypes such as boastful, egotistical, autocratic, and opportunistic. When the reverse happens, the resulting negative feminine stereotypes are weak, shy, submissive, fearful, inhibited, and nagging. The overaggressiveness of the male finds its counterpart in the passive aggressiveness of the female.

On Being and Becoming Human Together

In this concluding section, we come up against the most difficult question of all. Ruth Tiffany Barnhouse, a lay theologian and practicing psychiatrist, has written a stimulating article "On the Difference Between Men and Women."[27] In commenting on the difficulty of gender research, including the cultural biases of all such research, she uses the analogy of a magnifying glass. "But when the subject matter is the psyche itself, or any part of it, the problem is not unlike that of trying to look *at* a magnifying glass *through* a magnifying glass in order to find out what a magnifying glass *really* looks like." She further cautions that the result of such research must be used with great discretion because simply to discover what is, does not yet tell us what ought to be. The latter question is an even more difficult one although it is not one which can be avoided.

That we are in the midst of great changes in this area is abundantly clear. How shall the Christian community respond to and participate in these changes? Are there any theological principles to guide us as we attempt to answer the question of what ought to be?

We do well to recognize that there are powerful social forces at work calling for change. These forces are not a fad which will soon blow over and leave us in peace. Particular spokespersons and particular ideologies indeed will come and go but the underlying convergence of forces which have given rise to the present situation are more enduring. In his book, *The Christian Response to the Sexual Revolution,* David R. Mace identifies and discusses five contributing factors which have given rise to the revolution. They are (a) the scientific study of sex; (b) the collapse of the taboos; (c) the emancipation of woman; (d) advances in medical knowledge; and (e) the era of individual freedom.[28]

While the Christian faith has a conservative mandate, that is, a mandate to conserve God's gifts in line with his intentions, it also has a prophetic mandate arising out of the same consideration. Christianity should not be found to be the preserver of the status quo. In reading the early chapters of Genesis, we discover that among the first marks of civilization after the fall are clothing, work, thorns and thistles, pain in childbearing, and the rule of man over woman. Underlying our civilization from the outset are such realities as shame, pain, curse, weariness, sweat, and domination. This is not a very promising beginning for such an important undertaking. Who would want to be in the unenviable position of defending a social order based on these?

The biblical message through both testaments is clear in its insistence on the fundamental ambiguity of all human institutions and conventions. Not only do our worst creations like warfare, for example, bear the marks of sin but so also do our noblest efforts, including our religious and familial structures. Continually we must work to refashion them in the light of God's requirements for loving, nonexploitive relationships. We are accountable to God for the way we work together as male and female in carrying out the mandate we have been given to subdue the earth and have dominion over it, including the very shape of our partnership itself. Insofar as that partnership has been characterized by domination, competition, exploitation, stereotyping, hostility, and alienation, it has fallen far short of what God originally intended.

Paul King Jewett in his book, *Man as Male and Female,* identifies three schools of thought on the question of how maleness and femaleness are related to the concept of the divine image.[29]

In the image of God he created him; male and female he created them. Note that the phrase "male and female" stands in apposition to the phrase "in the image of God." What is the connection between these phrases?

37

The first position outlined by Jewett is that "the male/female distinction has nothing to contribute to our understanding of Man as created in the divine image" because "true humanity transcends sexuality" and we should be thinking in terms of "oneness, not diversity, in terms of unity, not polarity."[30] This position would be reflected by those who say, "Let's stop talking about man and woman as such and emphasize *person.*" One example would be found in Professor Janet Saltzman Chafetz's book, *Masculine, Feminine or Human? An Overview of the Sociology of the Gender Roles.* She states in the Preface to the First Edition, "My particular interest is in bringing about changes that will encourage males and females to explore and develop their human potentials more fully, as opposed to maintaining the stereotyped masculine and feminine roles foisted upon them by virtually every aspect of this society."[31] She states that she is concerned with "human liberation" and not merely with "women's liberation" though she supports that cause as well.

A second view stresses the similarity of male and female rather than their distinctiveness. They are essentially similar in that to both of them are given the dominion over and stewardship of the created order. The female shares equally with the male in this responsibility and in the dignity which goes with it, and this is what it means to be created in the image of God. This is the point of view of those who, while agreeing that male and female are different, would say we make too much of it and that we should emphasize how they are alike, not how they are different.

The third view sees maleness and femaleness as essential to being in the image of God. It is not only what they share in common but their differentness which is of vital importance *for it is in that differentness which belongs together that the image consists.*

Their fellowship as male and female is what it *means* to be in the image of God. One should not then subsume the question of Man's sexual duality under the rubric of marriage and the family.... While marriage is perhaps the most intimate form of human fellowship, it is not the most basic. Men and women may *become* related as husband and wife, and many do; but they *are* related as man and woman by virtue of God's creative act. To be Man is to be male *or* female, male *and* female.[32]

It is the belongingness, mutuality, complementation, and relatedness of maleness and femaleness which need each other for completion and fulfillment that are emphasized in this view. The "or" emphasizes different-ness; the "and" emphasizes the togetherness of male-ness and femaleness.

For Jewett, the male-female relationship is more basic and fundamental even than marriage. For it is our maleness and femaleness in which the divine image in us consists and not our being married or being unmar-ried. It is our maleness and femaleness which remind us inevitably and forcefully that we are creatures in relationship.

Professor Letty M. Russell, a leading exponent of feminist theology, objects to beginning as Jewett does with the creation accounts as "an unfortunate starting point for investigations of partnership. Not only is the meaning of the image of God ambiguous, but also the creation accounts of Adam and Eve lead to a very nar-row range of images for investigating the possibilities of relationships of women and men in partnership."[33] She notes that "all the various views mentioned in the Jew-ett typology present difficulties for Christian feminists who are seeking equality for women and men."[34] Russell suggests "beginning from the other end," that is, with the New Creation in Christ rather than with the Old Creation, in exploring the future of partnership, the title of one of her stimulating books on this subject. When we do, we discover that the meaning of the new humanity in Jesus Christ is experienced not first of all in our maleness/femaleness, in our sexuality, but in participation, service, giving and receiving, sharing, fellowship, that is, in partnership.[35]

While we may agree with Russell that it is not an easy task to discern the full significance of the image of God for the partnership of women and men, surely part of its meaning refers to their freedom to shape and reshape their physical and social environment, including the shape of their partnership itself. Change within limits is both possible and necessary. Unlike the rest of God's created world, men and women do not stand locked into the laws of nature. To some extent, they like the Creator in whose image they are created stand over against nature. They are invited to share in the governing of the rest of the created order. They are to carry on God's work of creating a culture to cover the face of the earth. They are to make the gardens and vineyards bloom and to realize the potential of the soil for growing food. They are to create a civilization, a society in which women and men can live at peace with each other and with their neighbors. They are to be fruitful and multiply, to have children and raise them for the glory of God!

In large measure, they have gained control over nature. Our ancestors, for example, have conquered the wilderness and woods of the North American continent and made them their home. They built dams to tame the rivers and change their course. Through irrigation they made even the parched places fertile. In our time, we have learned how to travel from one place to another at high speeds—on the ground and under the ground, on the water and under the water, in the air and even in space. Is it any wonder that that same spirit which has challenged the limits and boundaries of outer space should now be turning its attention to the inner space of women and men as well as the space between them?

Men and women are learning how to predict and control human behavior through the sciences of physiology, psychology, sociology, and the like. In great measure, they have at their disposal great power to determine what they are to become.

To be created in the image of God is to be created for fellowship with God and to share in the fulfillment of the purpose and intention of God for all that he has brought into existence. But it is also to have the potential for asserting one's independence, for taking one's own way, for setting oneself up in rebellion against God. The tragic story of human history is that more often than not, men and women have chosen their own way and suffered the consequences. Left to their own devices and rejecting their responsibility to their maker, they have exploited and ravaged not only their environment but each other.

This mutual exploitation of men and women is in itself sufficient incentive for the Christian community to call for change both in the stereotyped sex roles and in the structures which institutionalize and perpetuate them. To the various voices which are calling for revolution, litigation, consciousness-raising, political action, education, and the like, the Christian community adds another call as supplement and/or alternate, the call for repentance.

The Christian community will also bring its distinctive approach to bear upon the analysis of the problem. Far from complaining that the various critiques of male-female relationships have been too radical, it will assert that the critiques have not been radical enough. Most of the critiques have been inadequate because they fail to recognize that the whole system has been corrupted by sin. It is only when men and women together acknowledge their complicity in rebelling against God's intention for their partnership and repent of their sin that they will be truly liberated.

Not only are there distinctive Christian perspectives on the analysis of the human situation but also on the goal and direction of change. Many different illustrations of the new social order that is being advocated share one underlying assumption, that the fulfillment and the self-realization of the individual are the measure of all things. If the individual's well-being is enhanced by any given relationship or social grouping, well and good. If it is frustated by one's commitment to another, that commitment may be, indeed *must* be, withdrawn. It is the thoroughgoing individualism of this philosophy of life which stands diametrically opposed to the Christian way. An example of this philosophy of life is to be found in the following prophecy:

> Men and women will increasingly come together as independent human beings who truly love and respect one another's individuality, form close relationships, share together, and sometimes marry. This relationship will last until one or the other changes or moves geographically and they find it to be no longer tenable.[36]

Individualism in its extreme form denies that community is essential to human existence. Or in a more subtle expression of it, individualists are prepared to acknowledge the necessity of community and to enter into it but only on their own terms. Their understanding of community is a faulty one; they conceive of it not as contributing to, even constituting, their personhood but only as an impersonal arrangement by which some of the needs which they, *as persons in their own right*, must have satisfied. So far as marriage is concerned, such a person holds it to be simply a convenient arrangement, a legal and social contract which may be broken when his needs are no longer adequately met. The individualist is increasingly reluctant even to take on the formal obligations of such a contract, let alone the informal and unspoken obligations of a permanent commitment of intimacy.

Emil Brunner was fond of characterizing such a person as a modern Robinson Crusoe, that is, one who

> enters into community; he forms it as one who in himself is a complete man, a personality.... He unites himself to other such personalities on condition that it is he who determines whether or not the union shall exist; it is he who establishes the conditions and therefore, even in the union, remains a free lord over himself.[37]

The third interpretation outlined by Jewett of what it means to be created in the image of God is one which rejects the notion that any individual can be complete in and of himself/herself. It is our need for relatedness which causes us to reach out to seek the other. Sexuality is not a marginal aspect of human existence, nor is its significance limited to biological reproduction. It is central to our very existence as those who have been created in the image of God. Maleness and femaleness speak of relatedness, complementation, mutuality, and belonging. It is in relating that we exist at all, and it is in relating that we point to and participate in communion and fellowship which is the way in which God exists. Maleness and femaleness, masculinity and femininity are essentially complementary qualities. Any social engineering which fails to take into account this fundamental rhythm and harmony which God has built into our existence is bound to produce dissonance and chaos. Our efforts should be expended in the direction of enhancing our partnership as male and female to make of it something that is both effective and harmonious. Male and female are called to be partners in the stewardship of God's creation and joint heirs of the grace of life.

Conclusion

We have been examining the changing relationships between women and men and the changing understanding of what it means to be masculine and feminine. Male-female relationships provide us with heightened experiences of both agony and ecstacy. What God has intended as a good gift to us has frequently become a problem. We noted that in the drama of male-female relationships, there is a tension which at times has led to alienation between the sexes. At its best, however, that tension has led men and women to discover that they need each other. They have a profound partnership in the tasks of life and in the fellowship of the gospel.

Because their partnership is a living relationship rather than a mechanical one fixed for all time, it is always in process of growth and change. Some persons feel threatened by these changes whereas others see in them the possibility for new vitality for both partners and for the relationship itself. We have explored some of the research on gender role/identity to discover what are the possibilities and what are the limits when it comes to new role patterns and gender self-understandings. We have concluded that there are many rigid stereotypes which have hindered the fuller flowering of relationships between the sexes. At the same time, biological differences (particularly reproductive functions) do in fact make a difference in the area of gender role/identity. It may well be that we have allowed these biological differences and the social/cultural differences to which they have given rise to obscure the fact that both women and men alike are created in the image of God. Both alike are stewards over the rest of the created order and share in the dignity of that stewardship. In Christ, the walls that separate us from each other are broken down for we are all one in him.

Some of the advocates of liberation from the old stereotypes tend to perpetuate the alienation between women and men by seeing man as "the enemy" and "the oppressor." Some operate on the assumption that the greatest good is the self-realization and fulfillment of the individual, no matter what the social cost is in terms of family stability, for example.

But the search to find new patterns of relationship is not necessarily based on such secular assumptions. The pattern of male-female relationships is not fixed in concrete for all time; it is a living organism constantly in search of those nutrients which will enhance its life. God expects us to make the most of the gift of maleness and femaleness so that we may discover the richer, fuller, deeper significance of what it means to live in relatedness, complementation, mutuality, and belonging. Only as we do shall we discover the deeper levels of what it means to be created in God's image.

2
The Two Shall Become One Flesh: On the Covenant of Marriage

Have you not read
that he who made them
from the beginning
made them male and female,
and said,
"For this reason
a man shall leave his father and mother
and be joined to his wife,
and the two shall become one"?
So they are no longer two
but one.
What therefore God has joined together,
let no man put asunder.
Matthew 19:4-6.

This is the response of Jesus to the Pharisees who came to test him concerning his theology of divorce. He responds to them, quoting Genesis 1:27 and 2:24, by stating his theology of marriage instead. He goes behind the tradition that has developed over the centuries to the original intention of God that marriage is to be a permanent covenant of fidelity between a man and a woman. We could wish that Jesus had said more on this, for it is a subject of vital interest and crucial importance especially in our time.

We noted in the first chapter that there is a sexual revolution under way. We are living in a time when all values regarding the way women and men live together are being reassessed. We have inquired into one dimension of that revolution, that is, the revolution in gender identity and sex roles. The key word in understanding the revolution is "liberation," that is, liberation from stereotyped expectations and behavior.

In addition to challenging the masculine/feminine stereotypes and the conventions and institutions which have been built up around them, the sexual revolution is advocating "liberation" from traditional patterns of sexual morality. Several of its more radical proponents have mounted a vigorous attack on the institution of monogamous marriage as archaic, outworn, and hypocritical. It is criticized as an ill-fated and inappropriate attempt to limit narrowly the flow of our erotic energies into a single channel. This, we are told, is a losing battle against nature which intends that these energies should flow into a number of streams and rivers, overflowing their banks, spilling and splashing generously, profusely, and joyously where they will.

A number of titles both describing and advocating "alternative intimate life-styles" have been published in the last few years by scholars holding academic appointments at major universities. The revolution in sexual roles and the revolution in sexual morality are in some respects twin expressions of a common philosophy in which individualism and self-realization are unquestioned values.

The Critique of Monogamy

The ideal of monogamous marriage, of permanent fidelity taught by Jesus, has been institutionalized in the marriage practices and laws of the Western world for many centuries. It has, however, not always been the normative model for marriage even in biblical times. Polygamy and concubinage were apparently acceptable forms of marital relation in early Israel though by the time of Christ only monogamy was socially and theologically approved. Fornication and adultery were forbidden; so also were sexual relations with a prostitute. It is obvious that monogamy as social policy has not been without its difficulties. Two institutions, one formal and one informal, were created to make it both endurable and enduring. The formal one was divorce which in recent times has been somewhat cynically dubbed "serial monogamy." That is to say, monogamy means having only one wife; serial monogamy means having only one wife at a time. The informal institution was known as the double standard which meant that although nice girls didn't, nice boys did but not with nice girls. It assumed that it was the prerogative of a young man to come sexually experienced to the marital bed; at the same time, he expected that his bride would come as a virgin.

The chastity belt was another expression of the double standard; a man traveling away from home could, according to the legends surrounding this bizarre costume, lock his wife into one and carry the key with him thereby ensuring that no one else would have sexual access to her during his absence. Apparently there was no male equivalent to the chastity belt.

The double standard arose out of prevalent cultural notions about male and female sexuality. Females were thought to be sensual but not sexual; since it was assumed that they had no sexual feelings or desires, there was no real deprivation in denying them the sexual freedom that some men claimed. The double standard was apparently widespread in Western society, but this is not to say that it was the majority view. Faithfulness in marriage on the part of men as well as women was also widespread and endures even into our times in spite of whispers and shouts to the contrary.

Nonetheless, monogamy is in for a hard time today and its detractors are becoming bolder. One wonders, however, if the critiques are focused upon the ideal set forth by Jesus, or upon the way it has been institutionalized by Western society. If it is the latter, who among us would not be prepared to join in the criticism of the somewhat grim, joyless, fragile, creaky, and even hypocritical institution our world seems to have made of it!

What are the critics saying about monogamy? They are saying that the rising incidence of marital breakup as indicated by the divorce rate is evidence that something is fundamentally wrong with our marriage system. It is not the people who have failed, they say, but the institution. The institution has failed because it is based on false assumptions and expectations. Among these erroneous expectations is the one that "all of one's personal, sexual and social needs can be met through monogamous marriage."[1]

The critics are also saying that there is scant support for two of the primary claims which are usually set forth justifying monogamous marriage, that it "specially promotes 'profound affection' between the partners or a 'loving context' for child upbringing. Such claims are simply without force," according to Professor John McMurtry of the University of Guelph, Ontario, in a sharply worded tract on the subject. He says that monogamous marriage is so taken for granted in our culture that we tend to assume uncritically that "it is dictated by the laws of God, Nature, Government and Good Sense all at once. Though it is perhaps unusual for a social practice to be so broadly underwritten, we generally find comfort rather than curiosity in this fact and seldom wonder how something could be divinely inspired, biologically determined, (legally) coerced, and reasoned out all at the same time."[2] He then proceeds systematically to dismantle the assumptions on which he says monogamy is based and to expose their fallacies.

It is a fallacy, in McMurtry's judgment, to assume that emotional intimacy can be fostered through a legal institution. It is a fallacy to assume that a loving context for bringing up children can be nourished in a setting where the adult partners are cut off by design from loving intimate relationships with other adults and thus from the emotional nurturance of their own lives. It is a fallacy to assume that a systematic exclusion of sexual access to other women and men will promote anything other than "conjugal insecurity, jealousy and alienation."[3] Such "strict restraint of sexual energies"[4] simply won't work; to fail to recognize this is actually to build in deception, suspicion, frustration, and destructive aggression as integral parts of the system. Society needs alternatives to monogamy which are more realistic about the human sexual drives and which do not place artificial barriers in the way of their expression.

Alternative Intimate Lifestyles

Among the alternative intimate lifestyles which are described in the book of which McMurtry's essay is a part are cohabitation, extramarital and comarital sex, sexually open marriages, swinging, group marriage, communes, and creative singlehood. Only monogamy suffers from a bad press in this treatment, one of several such anthologies which have appeared in the past few years.[5] Creative singlehood is understood as involving sexual independence, that is, the freedom to enter into sexual liaisons for shorter or longer periods of time without any expectation of permanence or exclusiveness; it does not take on the burdens of having to work out the whole complex of relationships that are involved either in marriage or cohabitation.

Cohabitation is defined by Charles Lee Cole, director of the Cohabitation Research Project, as a "more or less permanent relationship in which two unmarried persons of the opposite sex share a living facility without legal contract."[6] It is "a special type of primary relationship in which the partners meet socioemotional, sociosexual, sociophysical and socioeconomic needs and maintenance functions."[7]

Cohabitation is seen by many observers as an advanced stage in courtship, a kind of trial marriage, and as such the least threatening to the institution of monogamous marriage of all the alternatives under review. By far the large majority of cohabitants are sexually exclusive in their relationships although only a minority enter into the arrangement with a stated commitment to permanency. This does not mean that such commitment will never develop, for many such couples do eventually enter into a legal marriage. No statistics on the number are as yet available. It is, of course, the reluctance to make a permanent commitment at the outset of the cohabitation period which is the essential mark of this arrangement. Cole states that "it is evident from the data on commitment that most student cohabitants view the relationship as important and worth continuing only as long as it provides mutual satisfaction and enjoyment which they feel is rewarding enough to work for through their investment of self."[8]

The distinction between extramarital sex and comarital sex is a bit difficult to discern in the literature but it may hinge on the relative degree of knowledge and approval by the spouse of the other mate's outside sexual activity. Extramarital sex may be described as cheating or unfaithfulness whereas comarital sex is entered into by one or both spouses with other persons with mutual knowledge and consent. Sometimes this is called open marriage, a term first made popular in 1977 by George and Nena O'Neill in a book by that title. The O'Neills were not advocating sexual openness as part of their definition but did acknowledge that openness could theoretically include the sexual dimension in certain instances.

Since they published their book, others have advocated and practiced the concept of sexually open marriages. The practice ranges from transient relationships with little or no affection (known as swinging) to high and deep levels of commitment to the outside partner(s) (known as comarital sex) including in some instances shared living arrangements (known as group marriages). So far, the sheer complexity of managing the emotional and practical logistics of multiple primary arrangements has kept the number of group marriages rather small and has kept those that do exist from including more than three or four marital partners.

Christopher Lasch in his book, *Haven in a Heartless World,* makes a telling comment on the phrase "nonbinding commitments" which he says was "used by Nena and George O'Neill without any sense of its irony."[9]

> The ideology of nonbinding commitments, superficially optimistic about the power of positive thinking, radiates pessimism; it is the

world view of the resigned. Claiming to represent the future, it regards the future with dread, having given up the hope that technology can be controlled or the social order made more just. Loss of faith in the future implies a similar loss of hope that the past can serve as a guide to the future or even become intelligible. 'Living for now' is one of the main items in the therapeutic program.... The fear and rejection of parenthood, the tendency to view the family as nothing more than marriage, and the perception of marriage as merely one in a series of nonbinding commitments, reflect a growing distrust of the future and a reluctance to make provisions for it—to lay up goods and experience for the use of the next generation.[10]

There are two additional caveats to the unbridled experimentation in intimacy that is going on which are given space in the Libby and Whitehurst volume. The first is a surprise and I shall let the critic speak in his own words before I identify him. He refers to a book he himself edited called *Adventures in Loving*,

which has more than twenty articles by people between twenty-five and forty-five attempting different life styles from bigamy to group arrangements, orgies, triads and open marriages. However, the plain truth is the most of these experimenters or adventurers, as I call them, have only the faintest idea of how to make alternate life-styles which incorporate multiple sexual involvements really work on an emotional, interpersonal basis.[11]

He then identifies several books on the subject which, he says,

give lip service to an unreal, impossible world of sexual freedom coupled with I-gotta-be-me interpersonal relationships. Most of them seem to be unaware that sexual hedonism as a way of life may be possible in the animal world but will not work for human beings.[12]

The surprise is that the writer of these words is Robert H. Rimmer, the social utopian who is best known for his advocacy of plural marriage in such novels as *The Harrad Experiment* and *Proposition 31*. His critique of the alternative intimate lifestyles movement as a whole focuses at two points. One, the idea of nonbinding commitments, and two, its preoccupation with the self rather than with the other. Rimmer is so committed to the idea of commitment that he says one can be committed to a deep and permanent love relationship with more than one person at a time, possibly two or three, no more. He says that "the human time factor" works against the deeper interrelationship of more than three couples in a lifetime. Furthermore, he insists that the essence of the love relationship is not taking out of it what's in it for me (that is, a pragmatic balancing of rewards and costs) but "mental-sexual surrender" to the other. In other words, it is self-giving, not taking.

The other critique comes in a Counter-Epilogue by David and Vera Mace. They state that their "major complaint about this book is that it fails almost completely to identify the 'alternative' form of marriage that is most widely practiced, and most widely preferred, in our contemporary society."[13] That alternative is companionship marriage which emphasizes the quality of relationships, mutual affection, sympathetic understanding, and comradeship. In responding to the inadequacies of traditional monogamy, they prefer the option of remedying its defects through programs of marriage enrichment rather than abandoning ship in favor of other models.

As the Maces point out, there is little that is actually novel in the experiments in intimacy that are set forth in the book. They see these not as the wave of the future but as vestigial remnants of the past which society has for the most part abandoned in the evolution of the monogamous nuclear family. What is new is the kind of advocacy these experiments are now receiving. It is only in recent times, within the past decade, that academics holding chairs of sociology, psychology, and family studies in Canadian and American universities have made these phenomena the object of scholarly study. In some instances, they have actually set themselves up as advocates of these alternatives. This has given rise to a new genre of literature, one in which the processes and the language of objective social science are set within the framework of propaganda. As Cuber and Harroff say in the Foreword, "Like *Renovating Marriage* (its predecessor), this book breaks with the trite, genteel 'value free' tradition of so many social scientists. One always knows what Libby and Whitehurst, and their collaborators, advocate on each of the issues considered."[14]

The second thing that is new is the amazing tolerance of an increasingly pluralistic society. The media have prepared the way in softening up the general public which was initially shocked, then titillated and eventually bored and apathetic about the whole thing. What else is new? has become an increasingly characteristic attitude on the part of many.

The third thing that is new is the impact of science and technology upon both the knowledge and management of human sexuality. We have begun to see, though not to comprehend, the fuller implications of our ability to divorce sexual intercourse from procreation. As with other modern discoveries and creations so in this area, our technology, in so many respects a boon and a blessing, has outdistanced our wisdom to manage and control it. Though the potential of contraception to deepen the intimate dimensions of human sexual loving is clearly evident, so also is its potential for depersonalizing human sexual relations. It may well be the growing depersonalization of our society which is creating the sense of urgency some persons feel to find intimacy. Failing to experience it in one deeply committed relationship, they search for it again and again and again.

This may also account for a fourth aspect of the modern search for sexual intimacy. It is the strong antithesis that is set up between the personal and the institutional. With reference to sexuality and/or marriage, the emphasis is placed upon the subjective dimensions of the relationship (that is, love, affection, closeness, warmth) while the objective dimensions (that is, legal institutions and economic obligations) are ignored. The latter are seen not as contributing to but as actually hindering the full flowering of the loving relationship. A similar dualism is set up between the individual and social dimensions of the relationship. Society is seen as restrictive and oppressive in regard to the intimate life and as such its expectations, conventions, and sanctions may be rejected. These dualisms (between the subjective and the objective, the personal and the institutional, the individual and the social, the private and the public) are evidence, in my judgment, of the sexual alienation of our times.[15]

Marriage as Covenant

The notion of marriage as making promises is one which transcends these dualisms and holds forth the possibility of healing sexual alienation. There is a long marital tradition which comprehends within it the subjective and the objective, the personal and the institutional, the individual and the social, the private and the public, and heals these tensions and polarities. It is the biblical tradition of marriage as covenant. This is what James Burtchaell of the University of Notre Dame is referring to in the title and lead article of his book, *Marriage Among Christians: A Curious Tradition*. He sums up that tradition briefly in these words:

> Jesus surprised his followers by inviting them to a novel kind of marital commitment: for better or for worse, until death. It was an unremitting promise of fidelity, free of conditions on which one could and might withdraw, and it was the ground for both a more demanding love and a more secure trust. His followers found it a crazy sort of commitment, and he admitted it was, but said the

Father made it possible, just as he empowered men and women to quit their attachments to believe in and follow him.

This sort of commitment is desperately difficult to live up to, and older believers urge younger ones to approach these promises with care and caution. It being the decision of a lifetime, one has to plumb through the high feelings of affection to find a deeper, firmer ground to rest it on, and there is a wisdom about what are good grounds for marrying and what are unreliable ones.

The first times together bring their surprises, and it is a demanding task to smelt two persons into one household. Ironically, one cannot count on marriage changing one's partner's insufficiencies, yet that is exactly what one hopes from marriage.

Sex is meant to embody that surrender of privacy which comes from belonging to each other. It celebrates what marriage is, and has been given a deeper sense of joy by Christians who make these deeper promises. It is not best understood simply as an expression of love; rather, it embodies belonging—belonging in a way that only marriage quite achieves.[16]

Burtchaell acknowledges that this tradition will make sense only to those who accept the total vision of life which Jesus embodied and proclaimed. If persons choke on this view of marriage, they will undoubtedly choke on the larger theological framework of which it is an integral part. And central to that framework (both the larger one and the smaller one) is the idea of pledging not only one's word but one's very life to another. The key word is *covenant,* that is, *making promises.* Covenant is something like a contract but is different in that it makes no provision for an honorable dissolution. It is not limited or restrictive in its expectations and it leaves no back door partway open.

In setting forth this view of marriage as making promises, it is not our purpose to argue for the superiority of monogamous marriage in every respect. Indeed we can acknowledge the validity of some of the criticisms and the force of some of the arguments. We can certainly agree with the opening statement by Robert N. Whitehurst, who says, "As an idea, monogamy is beautiful to behold in its pristine philosophical purity; however, it is a little difficult to put the ideal into practice."[17]

We might even agree, though somewhat less cynically, with Bertrand Russell in his book *How to Be Happy Though Married,* published in 1885, which he dedicated to "those brave men and women who have ventured, or intend to venture, into that state which is a blessing to a few, a curse to many, and a great uncertainty to all." His advice to the newly married was to lower their unrealistic expectations of marriage and to enter into it with that same attitude with which some American pioneers entered into their new settlement, naming it Dictionary because "that's the only place where peace, prosperity and happiness are always to be found."[18] The point to be made is not that the biblical tradition of marriage as covenant is superior in such and such respects or that it is easy to live out. The point is that it is based on different assumptions and that one must come to terms with the foundations of the house of marriage, however it is built, and not only with the walls and the roof or the arrangement of the rooms. Only then will there be an adequate basis upon which one can make a choice among conflicting views.

The assumptions upon which the biblical tradition of marriage is built are made explicit in the following marriage vows:

> *Question:* (to both) Do you believe that matrimony is an ordinance instituted of God, confirmed and sanctioned by Jesus Christ, and that you must therefore enter upon it in the fear of God?
> *Question:* (to both) Do you confess and declare that you are unmarried and free from all other marriage relations and engagements whatsoever?
> *Question:* (to the groom) Will you, in the presence of God and these witnesses, take the sister by your side to be your wedded wife; will you love and cherish her, provide and care for her in health and in sickness, in prosperity and adversity, share with her the joys and sorrows of life, exercise patience, kindness and forbearance toward her, live with her in peace as becometh a faithful Christian

husband; and forsaking all others keep yourself only unto her as long as you both shall live?

Question: (to the bride) Will you, in the presence of God and these witnesses, take the brother by your side to be your wedded husband; will you love and cherish him, in health and in sickness, in prosperity and adversity, share with him the joys and sorrows of life, exercise patience, kindness and forbearance toward him and live with him in peace as becometh a faithful Christian wife; and forsaking all others keep yourself only unto him as long as you both shall live?

There are some for whom these words may sound quaint and archaic, a distant echo from the past relegated to the dusty bins and archives of history along with the phrase, "and thereto do I plight thee my troth."

There are other persons, however, for whom these words sound a familiar note, for unless they were too stunned and dazed on their wedding day to hear what was being said they will remember that these or similar questions were put to them and that in turn they answered, "I do," "I am," "I will." The words may indeed sound like something out of the past but the tradition behind them and upon which they are based reminds us that Christian marriage is based on making promises, on trust, one's pledged word, on covenant.

Emil Brunner, a European theologian now deceased, has said of marriage that "where marriage is based on love, all is lost from the beginning" and that "to build marriage on love is to build on the sand."[19] What Brunner meant by these rather dim words is that the bedrock upon which the institution of Christian marriage is built is fidelity. He was not, of course, denying that love is an essential ingredient of the marriage relationship (and notice that in the above marriage vows the content of the covenant is *to love* and *to cherish*). But love that is primarily a *feeling* rather than a *promise* can be fickle and inconstant. Love that thrives only by candlelight and moonlight and disappears when sickness comes or there are too many children and not enough money is not an adequate basis for the marriage relationship. What Brunner had in mind is that it is precarious for Christians to get their basic definitions from the world's values and understandings and that the only sure foundation for Christian marriage is faithfulness.

Sometimes I am asked, What is love? by persons who may genuinely desire to know, though sometimes it is asked in a manner similar to that of the lawyer in Luke 10 who asked, "And who is my neighbor?" On one occasion a young man asked this when I had asked him what his marriage vows had been and whether he had intended to keep them in the first place. He responded that he had indeed intended at that time to keep them but at that time he was in love. When I pressed him as to what had happened to that love and how it was that he was now released from its obligation, he asked me, "What *is* love?" One answer I sometimes give is that it is similar to Harry Stack Sullivan's definition of maturity which is the ability to regard someone else as of equal worth to yourself, or nearly so, and to give equal weight to their needs and desires as to your own.[20] That is indeed a high standard.

The Analogy of the Church as the Bride of Christ

The apostle Paul in Ephesians 5:21-33 compares the husband-wife relationship to the union between Christ and the church. This analogy should not be pressed too far or interpreted too literally to make it say what Paul did not intend. We may, however, safely infer that the inner connection which brings these two relationships into a common orbit is the spiritual union between the parties, that is, the union of mind, heart, and spirit; of values, intention, and destiny.

This analogy points out that the essence of the marriage relationship is to be found in covenant, a covenant that is both similar to and in some respects participates in the covenant between Christ and his church. In terms of its practical expression, the key elements in both covenants are love and faithfulness. A marriage covenant that is entered into soberly, joyfully, and in the fear of God (a marriage covenant to which Christ becomes a party and in which he is a continuing presence and witness) is certainly something more than a legal contract for it does not hedge its commitments in the fine print nor specify under what conditions it may be abrogated. It bears within it the essence of communion and community as surely as does that little group of two or three of whom Christ said that he is in the midst of them if they are gathered in his name. For this reason, some theologians have begun referring to the family created on the basis of Christian covenant as "la petite église," the little church.

A covenant relationship is firm, final, and permanent; it cannot be terminated, only violated. Violating it rips and tears apart that unity of life which has been sealed by God himself, "What therefore God has joined together, let no man put asunder." The basic pattern of the covenant relationship is to be seen in the covenant making ceremony in Exodus 19 and repeated many times in the Old Testament. It emphasizes the exclusiveness of the relationship. ("You shall be my own possession among all peoples.") There are special benefits in the covenant and special expectations. There are disastrous consequences if it is profaned.

Another of the current criticisms of monogamous marriage is that it is based on ownership, that is, "the maintenance by one man or woman of the effective right to exclude indefinitely all others from erotic access to the conjugal partner."[21] The statement is correct on its face but it is based on a limited, even distorted concept of ownership. What is intended by the concept of "possession" in the Exodus covenant making is not making a thing (property) out of persons but quite the opposite, making a people out of things (slaves). The quality to be emphasized is not ownership, but belonging. Once the slaves had been "no people" but now they are the covenant people of God. It is in this new belongingness that their humanness is restored and respected.

We discover and realize our full personhood in belonging. The marriage covenant is one expression, though not the only one, of belonging; at its best it becomes not a jealous guarding of privilege but a depth giving and receiving of such intimacy that both partners are set free to share their lives and their love with others. This is something like open marriage but not in the sense of sharing sexual love in a conjugal way for it recognizes that such adultery adulterates the covenant.

A third criticism of monogamous marriage that is now being heard is that it makes marital breakup too destructive.[22] Again there is a measure of truth in this complaint. Since covenant does not make provision for failure in its conditions, any failure is necessarily tragic and painful. There are, of course, some marriages which are terminated by the parties in an amicable agreement to disagree and go their separate ways, sometimes even as friends. It is doubtful, however, whether a marriage based on covenant can be so amicably terminated. The grief which attends it is as deep and bitter as the grief of death (or more so) and the separating parties do well to mourn the death of their covenant relationship when resurrection eludes them. That is, of course, the good news of the gospel for covenant marriage, that resurrection is a possibility devoutly to be wished and striven for.

In the Old Testament we see the pain of the abandoned partner when Israel breaks covenant and goes whoring after pagan gods. Note again the aptness of the image and the appropriate parallelisms between the covenant of God with his people and that between a husband and wife. The book of Hosea is very vivid in the way it describes this harlotry and adultery of God's people. Gomer, Hosea's adulterous bride, bears three children: a son named Jezreel; a daughter named Not Pitied; and a son named Not My People. But God's love, like Hosea's love, pursues the covenant breaker and her offspring, and eventually his forgiving, pursuing love triumphs over her faithlessness and he says in Hosea 2:23, "And I will have pity on Not Pitied, and I will say to Not My People, 'You are my people'; and he shall say, 'Thou art my God.' " The faithfulness and forgiving love of a covenant making and covenant restoring God are to be a model for Hosea to follow and for all to emulate wherever covenant is violated.

We seem to have lost something in our time in terms of our understanding of marriage as covenant. It has shown up in my counseling with some persons who don't seem to comprehend a covenant self-understanding when things get a bit rocky in their marriage. We need not think of the permanence of the marriage covenant as a prison into which persons are locked for life but may view it as a source of stability, security, and strength to help tide us over the rough places. Our task is cut out for us; it is to teach our young people clearly the covenant nature and implications of the marriage relationship. There is plenty of biblical material available and if we can teach them in the context of a congregation that takes covenant seriously and nurture them in the context of families who take covenant seriously, we may yet prevail over a society whose values emphasize individualism, pleasure, and reluctance to make permanent commitments to others without reservations and conditions.

Of course I recognize that persons fail, marriages fail, and covenants are broken. I believe that the church can and must find ways to deal redemptively with persons and marriages that fail. I believe this can be done in the context of teaching the covenant nature of marriage and that the more effectively we do that, the less likely it is that we shall be faced in our families and congregations with marital failure. I use the term failure advisedly and not harshly; it is not an unloving act to recognize the truth for what it is, for only in this way can healing take place. The truth, however, includes the fact that not only did the covenanting couple fail in their covenant but so also did the larger covenant community which covenanted to nourish and nurture that covenant which was made in its midst. This is hardly the occasion for a pharisaic display of self-righteousness nor for neurotic breast beating and finger pointing; it is rather the occasion for therapeutic confession out of which all true healing is born.

Mutual Subjection in Love

The basic pattern of relationship in a marriage based on covenant is *mutual subjection in love.* The word *agape* has by now become part of our common vocabulary and to some degree it has become part of our lifestyle, but the fuller, richer, deeper significance of *agape* is for most of us still to be discovered. For *agape* we do not have only a definition (to love selflessly, without reservation); we have a model in the way Christ loves the church. "Husbands, love your wives, as Christ loved the church and gave himself up for her, that he might sanctify her, having cleansed her by the washing of water with the word, that he might present the church to himself in splendor, without spot or wrinkle,

64

or any such thing, that she might be holy and without blemish. Even so husbands should love their wives as their own bodies" (Ephesians 5:25-28a).

There are in these words two challenges, a major one and a minor one. The minor one is to love your wife as much as you love yourself. That's the standard referred to in Sullivan's definition, a high standard indeed but it still falls short of *agape*. That one is at least possible from a human point of view though it is rare and it is very difficult. The major challenge is to love like Christ, who gave up his life for his bride. Who has ever loved like that?

When I was a young fellow, I participated in the youth group of my church. Part of the fun of the evening's program would be to crack jokes at the expense of someone in harmless ways and so let everyone in on the secret of who was escorting whom. One evening shortly after Ruth and I had been seen in each other's company, a spurious letter which I had allegedly written to her was read to the entire company. It went as follows: "Dearest Ruth, I would climb the highest mountain for you. I would swim the widest ocean for you. I would cross the hottest desert and blaze a trail through the deepest jungle. Love, Ross. P.S. I'll be over on Saturday night if it doesn't rain." That silly thing has stuck in my mind because it has the ring of truth in it. I profess my love for her in brave and fearless tones. I think there is even some truth in it that given a desperate choice like rescuing her from a burning building at the expense of my own life or giving her the last seat on a lifeboat, I could and would rise to such a heroic gesture. The things I do find difficult arise in the everyday give-and-take of life at home, and there I must confess that I do not often rise to even the lesser challenge. It may well be, though, that they are the very setting where the greater challenges of *agape* living and loving are to be met.

Although the admonition to love as Christ loved is addressed directly to husbands, this applies equally to the wives who are similarly to love their husbands with that same quality of love. Likewise, husbands are not immune from the injunction given to wives to be subject to their husbands. I note, of course, that Paul develops the theme extensively of the wife's subjection to her husband in a way parallel to the church's subjection to Christ, and he asserts that the husband is the head of the wife as Christ is the head of the church. I also note, however, that the passage begins in verse 21 with the words that we are to be subject to one another out of reverence for Christ. Furthermore, the model and pattern for leadership is that given by our Lord, who did not lord it over others but stood headship on its head, so to speak. I do not believe that the models of leadership provided by the world where power and domination are exercised are of any guidance or help to us in working out the implications of this passage for the way a husband is to relate to his wife.

In discussing this very point, Paul King Jewett says that a marriage cannot be likened to an army. An army, being an impersonal structure created to do a specific task, tends to be run more along the lines of giving commands and exercising obedience.

In a true marriage, by contrast, rarely will either party command or obey, and when such occasions do arise one ought not to say the husband should always give the orders because he is a man or that the wife should always obey because she is a woman. Husbands are not to wives what generals are to privates. So to conceive the husband/wife relationship is to threaten marriage with tyranny on the man's part and artifice on the woman's part ... but if the man and the woman are partners in life, then they should share the responsibility of basic decision making in the human enterprise. And should a particular man and a particular woman become husband and wife, they too should make the basic decisions jointly. When mutual agreement cannot be achieved, the husband's preference should be honored by the wife in some instances, and the wife's by the husband in other instances.[23]

Jewett makes it clear that he is not arguing against the need for authority, obedience, hierarchy, superordination, and subordination in society. In fact, he notes that social structures would collapse if these were missing. He simply wishes to challenge the notion that in every situation in life women should be subordinate to men. The situation must define who is subordinate to whom rather than that in every instance it will universally be the case that the female is to be subordinate to the male.

> Men and women are persons related as partners in life. Hence neither men nor women by nature are born to command or obey; both are born to command in some circumstances, and to obey in others. And the more personal the relationship between them, the less there is of either; the less personal the relationship between them, the more there is of both.[24]

There is, it is true, a strong concern in the writings of Paul, the apostle, for social order, stability, authority, and submission. Paul's vision of the way things are going to be in the kingdom which God in Christ is bringing about even now and also in the age which is to come is described in the first chapter of Ephesians. It is a social order in which the chaos of rebellion and discord are replaced by the unity and harmony which come about by the submission of all things to the rule of Christ. The spiritual struggle which is at the heart of the drama of the gospel revolves around this very issue. When God's pattern is defied, brokenness and misery in every sphere of life are the result. When it is obeyed, fellowship and community are created.

Many interpreters of the New Testament are struggling with such texts as the one in Ephesians 5 in the light of the current agenda on liberation. They are having a difficult time with Paul on the issue of freedom and equality between women and men when they compare such texts as this one and particularly 1 Corinthians 11:2-16 and 14:34-35 with the bold assertion of Galatians 3:28 that in Christ there is neither male nor female. Some attempt to harmonize these apparent conflicts by distinguishing between those texts which are undeniably Pauline from those which are not. Some write him off as inconsistent, apparently with the assumption that it is necessary for Paul to say the same thing in every situation in order to maintain his credibility. In other words, they find it impossible to affirm with Paul both women's equality with men and subordination to men at the same time.

Jewett proposes to resolve this dilemma by observing that Paul's theological interpretation is shaped in part by his grasp of the new leaven of the Christian gospel and in part by the cultural background of Judaism in which Paul's life and thought are steeped. In other words, the old and the new are mixed in his teaching. Theologically Paul had become a Christian but culturally he still remained Jewish to a large extent. He has himself not yet fully comprehended the fuller implications of his own radical teaching about the relationship between women and men as set forth in Galatians 3:28.[25]

While it is not totally improbable that this may indeed be the case, we should first of all disabuse ourselves of the notion that only those things which are totally congruent with each other may be accepted as credible. Time and again the Christian church has stumbled in trying to resolve the dialectic tension between apparently mutually exclusive affirmations. Examples which come readily to mind have to do with the relationship between law and gospel, love and justice, and the divine and human natures of Christ. Do we know the truth of the matter of any of these when we have reconciled their intrinsic tension by coming down heavily on one side of the issue to the exclusion of the other so we need wrestle with the polarity no longer? My own view with respect to the present topic is that the freedom that women are to find in Christ and in their relationships with men, specifically wives with their husbands, is emphasized on the one side of the dialectic. The concern for social order, stability, and authority (internal), and for the good reputation of the church and the spread of the gospel (external) are emphasized on the other hand.

There was an early emphasis in Paul's writing (Galatians) on the freedom and the liberating power of the gospel. In implementing these principles in terms of changing the social structures, he discovered that sometimes he had to address himself to the excesses of the conservatives and sometimes to the excesses of the liberals. And neither, he despaired at times, fully comprehended all the implications of the new freedom Christ had wrought. In some sense it called for a delicate balancing act since his larger concern, even larger than his concern for liberation, was to unite Jews and Gentiles, not to alienate them. This was an even greater and more far-reaching social revolution than the revolution in male/female relationships. Among the great tragedies of Christian history is the fact that this social revolution at the very heart of the gospel itself has not yet been fully realized!

In the contemporary revolution in the relationship between women and men both in the family and in the larger society, most of the weight is being placed on the side of freedom rather than of stability. Much of the new freedom which women enjoy is to be welcomed and celebrated, but what if that freedom breaks down sexual fidelity and the stability of the family? Some revolutionaries support this breakdown openly for it is their belief that only then can a new just and loving social order be created. Is it possible for the Christian community to be concerned equally with affirming the fuller development and expression of the personhood of women (as well as men) while at the same time affirming the value of stability in our social and familial structures? In other words, can we maintain the dialectic tension between the subjective and the objective, the personal and the institutional, the individual and social dimensions of the issues before us? I believe that we can and that we must!

While it is true that much of the momentum in the modern liberation movement is scornful of Christian values, it is also true that not everything in the traditional ways of viewing male-female relationships arises out of concern for the gospel and is respectful of it. In each generation, the Christian community must discern what is the application of the new life in Christ to our cultural circumstances and social institutions which will best express the mind and will of Christ for our life today. We need not resent the nudge, shall I say the violent shove, that the liberation movements are giving us in the direction of rethinking our patterns but welcome them as a necessary incentive for exploring the implications of the good news of Christ for the way we live.

Henosis: Sexual Union in Marriage

So far we have interpreted the covenant of marriage in terms of a spiritual union, emphasizing such words as love and faithfulness. It would be a mistake, however, to interpret this passage in purely spiritual terms to the exclusion of the physical. Paul in appealing to the Genesis 2:24 passage, "Therefore a man leaves his father and his mother and cleaves to his wife, and they become one flesh" (Ephesians 5:31, quoting Genesis 2:24), is of course referring to a sexual union in which two persons are united into one. The term *henosis,* although it is not used in the New Testament itself, is a Greek word which has become a significant category in current theological discussions about the meaning of the marriage relationship.[26] It refers to the union in one flesh. The word came up a few years ago in the conflict on Cyprus in which the Greeks were pressing for the *henosis* of the two parts of the island, Greek and Turkish, into a political union.

Paul uses the same phrase in 1 Corinthians 6:16 but here the usage is difficult and somewhat problematic. It refers in that instance to the sexual union of a man with a prostitute. Is that union to be thought of as in some sense a marriage? I do not think so, even though it shares an essential ingredient with marriage, that is, sexual union. However, the covenant of love and faithfulness and the spiritual unity described in Ephesians 5 are not present. We must therefore conclude that it is not the sexual union itself but the covenant which surrounds it giving shape to the nature and quality of the relationship which is the essence of marriage. Covenant is the unique and distinguishing characteristic which makes marriage truly marriage in the Christian sense. We need to understand the context of the sexual union in order to assess its meaning and its quality. One modern view of sexual intercourse holds that it is nothing but a physical act with no moral significance; it is simply a necessary bodily function like eating and drinking. The Christian view holds that the physical act calls into play spiritual, moral, emotional, and social considerations which help to define the act as good or as something else.

Gibson Winter calls the covenant of union in one flesh the covenant of intimacy. The basic human need, in his analysis of the human situation, is the need for intimacy; in marriage and the family (and particularly in the sexual act) the need for intimacy is most nearly satisfied. "The sexual act conveys solidarity, intimacy, mutual concern, the surrender to one another. It expresses intimacy in the fullest and deepest sense."[27] Unfortunately, the contemporary social and cultural environment, says Winter, has robbed us of our capacity for achieving intimacy at the same time that it has increased our need for it. As a result, "the breakdown of intimacy in marriage empties the sexual act of its substantial meaning. Sexuality without mutual intimacy is counterfeit."[28] D. S. Bailey calls sexual intercourse of this kind a "hollow, ephemeral, diabolical parody of marriage which works disintegration in the personality and leaves behind a deeply seated sense of frustration and dissatisfaction. . . ."[29]

Winter does not advise married couples to abstain from conjugal relations until they effect a more satisfactory personal relationship since "sexual intercourse is not simply an expression of intimacy. It is at the same time a means of deepening and strengthening intimacy."[30] Bailey asserts that "it involves ... the whole being, and affects the personality at the deepest level. . . . It implies the resolution of discord, the transcending of superficial differences and antagonisms at a new and deeper level of existence or experience."[31]

A fourth objection which is being raised to traditional monogamous marriage is that intimacy cannot be legislated. Roger Libby, for example, asserts, "Although our often repressive legal and economic-political system make it more difficult to achieve intimacy, the search for intimacy is likely to be enhanced by social movements identified in this book [*Marriage and Alternatives: Exploring Intimate Relationships*], and the law and other traditional institutions will have little impact on genuine feelings and experiences."[32]

That one cannot legislate genuine intimacy nor

guarantee it by a marriage certificate cannot be disputed but that is hardly the point at issue. Sometimes the question is asked, When does a marriage begin, when the vows are said or in the marriage bed? While acknowledging that the union in one flesh (sexual intercourse) is an essential part of the definition of marriage, we cannot find that it in itself is definitive. There is too much of the subjective and the contingent in it to allow it to carry all that freight of meaning. On the other hand, nor do we find the definitive element in marriage to lie in its legal or institutional character.

John Meyendorff accepts the ancient principle of Roman law that "marriage is not in the intercourse but in the consent" and goes on to say that "the essence of marriage lies in the consent which in turn gives meaning and legal substance to the marriage agreement or contract."[33] In other words, it is not that the law gives meaning to the consent but that consent is what gives the contract its legal substance and force. In turn, the law must be assured that the consent is valid and not coerced or granted without the necessary capacity to do so (for example, by a child or a feeble-minded person who may be unaware of the implications of their act). Meyendorff notes that the Christian church both before and after the arrangement with Constantine accepted and found no reason to reject the legal and contractual arrangement set by the state for marriage. It acknowledged the valid interests of the state in determining who had a right to marry and in maintaining a record of these marriages.

At the same time, the church never accepted the legal definition of marriage as expressing its full essence. That is to say, conformity to the laws of the state with regard to marriage did not imply that the church accepted the state's legislation as *the* definition of marriage.

What mattered therefore was not the particular ceremony used to conclude the marriage but who was accepting the marriage contract. If the parties were Christian, the marriage was a Christian marriage involving Christian responsibility and Christian experience. For them marriage was a sacrament, not simply a legal agreement.[34]

We have preferred the term covenant to the term sacrament. This is especially the case in light of the technical usage of the term as it is developed in the theology of the Orthodox Church of which Meyendorff is a spokesman. The basic point he is making, however, is a valid one. We do not find the essential meaning of marriage either in the subjective dimension alone nor in the objective, institutional dimension alone. Rather we find it in its covenantal character which comprehends all the various dimensions of marriage within it and gives them their essential unity.

Conclusion

In this second chapter, we continued the theme of the Christian response to the sexual revolution by extending the analysis and critique to a second aspect of the revolution, that is, "liberation" from traditional patterns of sexual morality. We have taken note of the vigorous attack on the institution of monogamous marriage. The critics are saying (1) that it is a beautiful ideal but hard to live up to; (2) that it is based on ownership; (3) that it makes marital breakup too destructive; and (4) that in any case intimacy cannot be legislated.

In response, we have set forth an alternative perspective by which to view the marital relationship, the model of Christian marriage based on covenant in which each person seeks not first of all his/her own good but that of the covenant partner. We have agreed with the critics that monogamous marriage is an ideal difficult to live up to but have also agreed with James Burtchaell that

Christ gives grace to make it possible. We have disagreed with the critics on the point of ownership, stressing that it is *belonging*, not *ownership*, that is the essence of covenant and that it is in belonging that our true human dignity is celebrated. We have agreed with the critics that marital breakup is indeed costly in every respect but have asked how it could be otherwise. We have also agreed that intimacy cannot be legislated but asserted that that is hardly the point at issue.

Marriage is a socio-legal institution within which an authentic *henosis* or sexual union may be expressed. The institution of marriage is, of course, not a guarantee that the sexual union will be authentic or that it will not be betrayed. Simply to build an institution around a relationship does not necessarily bring with it an appropriate channeling of all the moral, spiritual, and emotional factors which attend such an intimate union.

However, marriage and the family are a system of intimate relationships which need the protection and support which society with its laws and its structures can provide in order to survive. At the same time, we recognize that these are only the shell and not the kernel. The shell represents the objective, institutional dimensions of the marriage covenant which surround and give long-term support and shape to the intimate union of the marriage partners in terms of social, economic, and legal obligations. Society cannot create that intimate union nor can it guarantee its survival. It can only acknowledge its presence through its marriage laws and its death through its divorce laws.

The inner kernel represents the marriage covenant viewed in its subjective, interpersonal dimensions: the sexual union and the physical, emotional, psychological, and spiritual texture of that union.

We may visualize the various dimensions of the marriage covenant in diagrammatic form in terms of a sphere or a round ball. The inner core of the sphere represents the marriage covenant viewed in terms of the subjective, the personal, the individual, and the private dimensions of the covenant. They characterize the union in its sexual, physical, emotional, psychological, and spiritual expressions.

The outer covering of the sphere represents the marriage covenant viewed in terms of its objective, institutional, social, and public dimensions. They characterize the union in its legal, economic, and social expressions. The texture and design of the outer shell are less important than that they in fact protect the inner core.

All of these dimensions and expressions of the marriage union are comprehended in the marriage covenant which nonetheless transcends the totality of all of them together. The marriage covenant is not merely their sum total. It is the participation and the presence of Christ within this earthly relationship which sets it apart from other human relationships and institutions and elevates it to covenant status.

The concept of covenant set forth in Ephesians 5 comparing the husband-wife relationship to that between Christ and the church both transcends and comprehends the interpersonal and the institutional dimensions and gives them a new quality and character. That quality and character are best expressed as love (in the sense of loving selflessly) and faithfulness. Where love and faithfulness are dominant in the relationship, you truly have covenant and in that covenant the two truly become one.

3
Be Fruitful and Multiply: On the Community of the Family

And God blessed them,
and God said to them,
"Be fruitful and multiply,
and fill the earth and subdue it;
and have dominion
over the fish of the sea
and
over the birds of the air
and
over every living thing
that moves upon the earth."
Genesis 1:28.

These words following hard on the heels of the text in Genesis 1:27 which speaks of being created in the image of God, male and female, would seem to be a commentary on and elaboration of that theme. The issue of fecundity, the major issue in the verses immediately following, is of central significance in our time as well. These words about plants and trees yielding seed, and beasts, birds, and fish reproducing themselves remind us that we live in a sexual universe. Not only do we as women and men live in a sexual universe but we are ourselves part of that sexual process. In participating in that process as procreators, that is, as those who bring children to birth, we participate with God in his purpose of peopling the earth.

What is even more striking in this text, however, than the command to fill the earth is the command to subdue it, a dignity, it should be noted, that applies equally to women as to men. In one sense women and men stand within and participate in the sexual, reproductive process along with the fish of the sea, the birds of the air, the plants and the trees that grow in the soil, the beasts of the earth, and every living thing that creeps on it. In another sense, they stand apart from it and carry some responsibility to manage that process in ways that make human reproduction something other than the instinctive or automatic breeding of the animal world, for example. It is in this consideration that many Christian thinkers find theological justification for human intervention in the ecological system and for contraception in human reproduction.

We have briefly examined the impact of the sexual revolution on gender identity/roles and on monogamous marriage. The advocates of the revolution are determined to "liberate" us from stereotyped gender roles and from restrictions imposed on our freedom to express our full sexual energies in a variety of relationships. The more radical of the liberationists propose also to liberate us from the "bondage" of having and raising children. In the words of Margaret Sanger, the pioneer of the modern movement for birth control, "The problem of birth control has arisen directly from the effort of the feminine spirit to free itself from bondage ... it is woman's duty as well as her privilege to lay hold of the means of freedom.... Others may help, but she and she alone can free herself."[1]

Shulasmith Firestone goes one step (or perhaps several) further than Sanger in insisting that the "tyranny of the biological family" be broken altogether in the overthrow of the sex role system itself as the final goal of the liberationist movement. It is not simply male privilege which must be ended but the very social structures which divide society into public and private or domestic spheres; the former are assigned primarily to men and the latter primarily to women. Fundamental to that division is, of course, the female role in reproduction which ties the woman to the home and interferes with her functioning freely in the world of work and public affairs. In discussing her vision of a world without sex distinctions, she says,

The reproduction of the species by one sex for the benefit of both would be replaced by (at least the option of) artificial reproduction: children would be born to both sexes equally, or independently of either, however one chooses to look at it; the dependence of the child on the mother (and vice versa) would give way to a greatly shortened dependence on a small group of others in general, and any remaining inferiority to adults in physical strength would be compensated for culturally. The division of labour would be ended by the elimination of labour altogether (cybernation). The tyranny of the biological family would be broken.[2]

On Bearing and Rearing Children

Contraception is one of the controversial issues debated in the Roman Catholic world particularly during the time (fall of 1980) that the Vatican convened a Bishop's Synod on the Family. The working document for the synod, "The Role of the Christian Family in the Modern World," quotes the papal encyclical *Gaudium et Spes* on this text (Genesis 1:28) as follows, "In this phrase is found both God's gifts and the married couple's duty: in it is the beginning of human history and the possibility of dominating the whole of the earth." The document also quotes the teaching on this subject of the encyclical *Humanae Vitae*. Though recognizing that some regulation of births through "natural" methods is appropriate, it reiterates the teaching of the second Vatican Council that "the sons and daughters of the Church may not undertake methods of regulating procreation that are found blameworthy by the teaching authority of the Church in its unfolding of God's law." Although this continues to be the official position of the church, there is growing evidence that its sons and daughters are making use of all the modern methods of contraception that are practiced by their sisters and brothers outside the Catholic Church.

Non-Catholics tend to dismiss the traditional Catholic view on contraception as out of date and overly preoccupied with the assumptions of natural theology. Even Father Burtchaell of Notre Dame has been mildly critical of Pope Paul's encyclical on birth control in which "he called rhythm 'natural' and contraception 'artificial.' "[3] However, Burtchaell speaks not only for the Catholic tradition but also for the whole Christian theological tradition until recently when he ties the sexual act to procreation. He says, "It matters less whether any single act of sex be open to conception than whether the entire sequence (not of a month but of a lifetime) of giving and sex and marriage be open to family."[4] It is only in our time with the development of modern methods of contraception that it has been possible to separate the questions of having sex and having children and treating them as though they were in fact distinct questions. It is this divorce that has moved sex out of the context of marriage and the family and given impetus to a new sexual morality based primarily on pleasure rather than oriented in mutual responsibility for bearing and rearing children.

That is not to say that the idea of sexual pleasure within marriage has always been foreign or offensive to Christian thought. However, the Christian sexual tradition (for that matter the entire Western cultural tradition) has struggled with intense ambivalence about sex. The sexual drive has been recognized as a powerful one and three main strategies have emerged throughout history in terms of how to manage it, according to James B. Nelson. They are to control it (by reason and will), to ignore it, or to release it.[5] Paul in 1 Corinthians 7 suggests subordinating it to a higher cause (the kingdom of God) but recognizes with a sigh that not all have the gift of continence as he has and for such "it is better to marry than to burn" (1 Corinthians 7:9). Even Luther, a strong advocate of marriage, called it an "emergency hospital for the illness of human drives."[6] But all Christian thinkers, however they came to terms with the fact of powerful sexual drives, legitimized sexual intercourse (only in marriage, of course) as God's provision for peopling the earth.

Roland Bainton, not unmindful of the historical tendency in the church to regard sex and marriage with suspicious reserve, traces the positive aspects of that tradition which coexisted with the other and summarizes the basic consensus which prevailed.

> The Church then from the outset and throughout her history and in the midst of her own divisions has consistently taught that marriage is good, ordained of God for the propagation of the race,

sex is not evil, marriage should be to a single partner and for life. Both parties are obligated to be faithful to the bond.

With this common ground, diversities of emphasis were possible and have occurred. Sometimes, to be sure, the variations have become aberrations and, though claiming to be Christian, have been condemned by the Church at large. But apart from eccentricities there have been diversities, all validly Christian. They consist in an overemphasis upon some legitimate aspect of marriage. In an ideal relationship, all the variants are combined.[7]

He traces three views of marriage, each of which predominated in the Western world in turn until about the seventeenth century: the sacramental, the romantic, and the companionable. The sacramental view emphasized the religious nature of the marriage relationship stressing faithfulness and permanence. The romantic view, a later development in the tradition, had the effect of counterbalancing the depreciation of sex and marriage and exalted love as an essential ingredient of the marriage relationship as well. The sacramental view of marriage was that it served as the instrument of procreation and as a "remedy for sin." In the romantic movement, originally a secular movement and one which in its origins glorified adultery, the background, according to Bainton, was being prepared for understanding marriage in terms of the personal relationship between the spouses.

A third view of marriage is the "companionable where the emphasis is placed upon partnership in a common set of ideals and aspirations and a common endeavor."[8] It is particularly among the Puritans, Anabaptists, and Quakers that Bainton finds evidence of a deep mutual regard and a genuine partnership in the service of Christ and in the common tasks of life.[9] The care of the partners to subordinate their relationship to their religious vocation resulted in the enhancement of that relationship into a genuine mutuality.

The fact that the church for the most part disapproved of sexual intercourse outside the marital relationship and even then viewed it within the larger framework of children and family does not mean a lack of appreciation for sexual pleasure. At the heart of the Christian critique of recreational sex is that it is a shrunken act in which some vital dimensions are missing by definition. Moreover, the creative tension between pleasure and responsibility, affection and fidelity is destroyed.

Otto Piper sees in the biblical use of the verb "to know" to indicate sexual intercourse a profound awareness of the deeper significance of sex. He distinguishes between objective knowledge and comprehending knowledge; the knowledge gained through sexual experience is of the latter kind.

> It is an intuitive knowledge given in and with the sexual experience; it discloses what was thus far hidden from the individual; and its subject matter is one's self seen in the mutual relationship in which it stands with the partner's self.[10]

This knowledge, which can be communicated only by one's sexual partner, discovers to the individual the hidden meaning of masculinity or femininity—why it is that in order to exist one must exist as a man or as a woman, as the case may be; it is an "intuitive self-understanding." This understanding of the self is at the same time an understanding that personal existence is an existence in mutuality and dependence. One's masculinity or femininity, i.e., one's personhood, is realized in responsible relation to the complementary quality in another. Union in one flesh is a "fusion of the two individuals into a mutuality of existence, a common destination for reciprocity of life and experience."[11] The real occasion of pleasure in sexual intercourse is the "fact that the original antagonism implied in sexual differentiation is resolved when at the peak of the union all consciousness of difference vanishes."[12]

Piper says that this experience imparts more to the sexual partners than the awareness of their manhood and womanhood; since both are aware of the procreative character of sexual intercourse, even though it may not constitute their motivation for coming together, sexual union also imparts to them an existential awareness of their fatherhood and motherhood.

The likelihood that test-tube babies and artificial or surrogate wombs will displace the natural method of procreation as proposed by Firestone is not very great even though it is already technically possible. However, the conviction that the full equality of women with men is not possible until women enjoy the same benefits and accept the same responsibility for the public sector including the world of work that men do is more widely shared. The 1968 report to the United Nations on "The Status of Women in Sweden" stated that "the idea that women must be financially supported by marriage must effectively be opposed" since it gets in the way of their economic independence. While men should not be expected to support their wives financially, they should share equally with their wives in the financial support of their children and in rearing them as well.

Child rearing, even more than childbearing, is seen as an obstacle to women taking their rightful place in the world of work. So long as this is considered primarily their responsibility, they will not be able to compete with men for jobs and pay on an equal basis. Although the climate of public opinion is increasingly supportive of the desirability of a greater involvement by fathers in child nurture, public policy has not yet arrived at the place where paternal leaves are as freely granted as maternal leaves. What has emerged instead is a number of alternatives to parental child rearing such as child care centers in almost every city and town and a few experiments in communal family living arrangements similar to the Hutterite colony and the Israeli kibbutz.

Even in Sweden, however, there is a substantial body of opinion that is concerned about this trend in child rearing practices as articulated, for example, by Inger Rudberg:

> The question of the care and upbringing of children is the crux of the whole sex role debate, which should really be called the child debate, since it is the children who in the last resort are most concerned. Not all parents regard day nurseries as the ideal way of caring for their children. They think that for the mother, with the father's economic support and interested assistance, chiefly to take care of her children represents an irreplaceable value. This is a view and an evaluation which should be respected. It is not so much a question of the economically measurable uses of a mother in the home; it is a question of quite other values—of her personal contact and being together with her children, giving them security and values on which to build the life which awaits them. How many of a three-year-old's little questions and reflections are never raised in the boisterous atmosphere of a day nursery? Is it really so hard to understand that there are other values in life than those which consist in doing something useful, something which can be measured in money?[13]

One of the chief complaints about the traditional division of labor into the private and public sectors is that the basic rewards are to be found in the public sphere. Chafetz points out that homemakers receive no salary, only an allowance. This is money allocated to household expenses, not directly related to their investment of energy and creativity. That investment, she notes, has no publicly recognized market value since it is not calculated into the gross national product. Moreover, when domestic services are contracted for pay they are paid for at the lowest possible level. Homemaking is not only unpaid or underpaid; it conveys no social status or prestige. It does not provide for a sense of achievement, personal fulfillment, or success except in small private ways. Nor does it contribute to a woman's economic independence. These are among the rewards which society offers in the world of work and that world with its rewards belongs primarily to men.

Increasing numbers of women, including married women, have entered the world of work outside the home in recent years. In 1947, women 16 years old and over constituted 28.1 percent of the civilian labor force in the U.S.; in 1980 they were 42.4 percent of the total. The total number of employed women in 1947 was 16.7 million; in 1980 it was 44.3 million.[14] In spite of this dramatic increase in the number of women working, it is still the case that women are largely confined to the lower paid positions. On September 2, 1981, a report documenting that women are "systematically under-paid" was released by the Equal Employment Opportunity Commission. Sociologist Ann R. Miller of the University of Pennsylvania, who headed the research panel, stated that

> despite the tremendous changes that have occurred in the labor market over the past 20 years, there has been no change in the relative earnings of men and women. In the early 1960's, women who worked the whole year at full-time jobs earned less than 60 percent of what men did and that is still true today.[15]

Small wonder, then, that women complain that even though they are finding greater opportunities to work outside the home, the rewards associated with such opportunities still elude them. Sexist discrimination is still very much alive!

Even if such discrimination is eventually ended, we are still left with the question of how worth is measured. Granted that a male-oriented society measures it in terms of money and what goes with it (power, prestige, status, recognition, etc.), do we not have a right to expect more from the liberation movement than an uncritical acceptance of these values? More to the point, where is the Christian movement's critique of such a social order? This is a time for all Christian women and men to examine their assumptions and their commitments. It is not a question first of all of whether women should have the right to be employed with job opportunities and pay equal to men. The answer to that question should be self-evident and it should be answered in the affirmative. The question is *how* both women and men should enter into the world of work and *how* their entrance together affects their participation as partners in the tasks of the home and in the nurture of their children.

One specific example of the question to be considered is what value is placed on the child in the home. Is the presence of children considered to be a hindrance to the personal self-realization of the mother and/or the father? Are children considered to be an economic liability? If that is the basic motivation for family planning or for having no children at all, Christians would do well to listen to another point of view. Increasingly persons from South America, Africa, and Asia are expressing resistance to the efforts of population planners who, they point out, are largely based in Europe and North America. While many of them recognize the actual and potential problems of a serious imbalance between the world's population and its resources of space, food, and energy, they are increasingly suspicious of the Western world's motivations in this regard. The West says that parents should have fewer children. The people in the developing countries say that the real problem is not overpopulation but overconsumption, especially by Europeans and North Americans. One philosophy of life says there should be fewer people so that each can consume more, that is, enjoy a higher standard of living. The other philosophy is that each person should consume less so that more people can enjoy a higher standard of life. One philosophy is oriented around things, the other around persons.

Both perspectives, it would seem, will have to be taken into account as the nations of the world develop a policy on population and family planning and as individual families determine the number of children they will have. This is a largely new question in human history for which there is little historical precedent to guide us. It should be noted again that the commandment of God included not only to fill the earth but to subdue it. This would seem to involve a harmonious coordination of the reproductive process with the management and development of the resources of the earth so that the people of the earth will be sustained.

The Socialization of the Young Child

We turn now to an even more urgent question than the question of whether or not to have children. That is the question of what to do with our children when they arrive, that is to say, the socialization process which many sociologists see as one of the few remaining functions of the family in modern society. As we have seen already, even that function may be assigned to other agencies in the world of the future if both women and men devote their energies primarily to the public sphere.

The socialization of the young child is no mean task in spite of the lack of social recognition that parents, especially mothers, receive for their efforts. Usually their recognition comes in the form of negative criticism of their inadequate efforts on the part of educators, therapists, theologians, and others. The transfer of family functions which has taken place over the years, what Christopher Lasch calls the "socialization of reproduction—the expropriation of parental functions by agencies outside the family,"[16] was not simply an inevitable result of social change. It was the direct result of a deliberate policy by social engineers of various kinds.

Today we see one of the few remaining functions of the family in process of transition, that is, the socialization of the young child. The rationale for this transition has already been traced, to free the mother for fuller participation in the labor force in order to gain economic equality with her husband. Only if she becomes economically independent, it is said, will she gain political, social, and legal equality. To achieve this, the young child will have to be nurtured primarily by others. However, we are told, we should not feel badly about this because mothers don't do such a good job of it anyway, especially if they are frustrated and unfulfilled because they are not out working for pay. It is a far better policy to turn this task over to those who are professionally trained and salaried. In this way, the dignity and status that should appropriately go with such a complex demanding task will be acknowledged as well.

There is much to be said for this point of view and I would not wish to be understood as downgrading the contribution made by many child care centers and their competent professional staff. There are situations where this represents either a better alternative or the only alternative. The basic question we are addressing is whether to support a social policy in which such programs become normative and replace the family's function rather than being supportive of and complementary to it. While there is no doubt that professionals are capable of loving small children, we must ask the question whether loving should be professionalized. After all, loving is of the essence in the socialization process.

What are we referring to when we speak of the socialization process? Lasch describes it as the "reproduction of culture" in which it becomes "embedded in personality."[17]

As the chief agency of socialization, the family reproduces cultural patterns in the individual. It not only imparts ethical norms, providing the child with his first instruction in the prevailing social rules, it profoundly shapes his character in ways of which he is not even aware. The family instills modes of thought and action that become habitual. Because of its enormous emotional influence, it colors all of a child's subsequent experience.

The union of love and discipline in the same persons, mother and father, creates a highly charged environment in which the child learns lessons he will never get over.... Parents first embody love and power, and each of their actions conveys to the child, quite independently of their overt intentions, the injunctions and constraints by means of which society attempts to organize experience.[18]

The family context is a powerful setting in which learning takes place in informal ways, that is, it takes place in the midst of living. Among the learnings which are of special importance are the development of a sense of identity, of belonging, of security, of personal worth, of the dignity and worth of other persons, of the capacity to make decisions, of the capacity for gratitude, of the capacity for relationships, of the value of animals and things, and an appreciation of the mystery, wonder, and sacredness of life.

The most obvious accomplishment of the young child in the family, an extremely complex one yet one that is taken for granted, is the development of language, that is, of hearing and speaking. The development of gender roles and identity is a second major accomplishment whose achievement has been compared to learning a language. Money and Tucker observe "that the critical period for gender identity differentiation coincides with the critical period for learning language," the first few years after birth.[19]

Not only do these two learning processes coincide in time, they proceed along similar lines. In each case, the infant is born with the capacity (for speech and for gender identity) but the particular language and the particular gender identity have to be learned. In the case of speech, it arises out of interaction with significant others who speak to the young child in a particular language. When learned, this is known as the native language or the mother tongue. The verbal and non-verbal symbols uttered in a social context of meanings are absorbed into an internalized fabric of meaning through the action of the ears, the eyes, the mouth, and the brain which organizes and stores them. In similar ways, the child develops a feminine or masculine self-understanding through interaction with both significant females and males (first mother and father) who "speak" to the child in the "language" of femininity and masculinity. The verbal and nonverbal symbols become internalized into a fabric of meaning.

It should be noted that very little of a parent's conscious thought and effort go into the task of shaping the growing child into a man or a woman. Most of it is subtle or implicit and takes place through modeling feminine or masculine behavior. However, a little girl learns about feminine behavior not only from imitating her mother, but also by observing her father's response both to her mother and to her. The technical term for her response to her mother's feminine behavior is *identification* and to her father's responsiveness is *complementary identification*.[20] Similar processes are at work as a little boy learns masculine behavior.

Concerning this interaction between parent and child, the question has been raised as to who acts as the stimulus and who as the response. The answer is that the parent-child relationship is such a complex system that it is impossible to tell. Is it because baby girls are more responsive to sounds that both mothers and fathers talk more to them and baby boys prefer being held to being talked to that they receive more cuddling? Or does it lie in adult notions of how male and/or female infants should be treated? In any case, it is clear from the beginning that baby girls and baby boys receive different kinds of treatment from both parents. Additional examples of this *differential treatment* are the clothes in which they are dressed, the toys they are given to play with, and the emotions which are encouraged or discouraged. It is in these areas that the socialization process tends to become more direct and explicit and is frequently accompanied by words clarifying the parents' expectations. Next to the influence of the parents and of brothers and sisters is the not insubstantial influence of grandparents who may confirm the other inputs or call them into question in line with their own ideas of masculinity and femininity.

In a myriad of ways, both implicit and explicit, both confusing and confirming, the message gets through to the child. By the end of the third year he/she has a fairly fixed notion of himself as a boy or herself as a girl. This notion gets elaborated and/or modified by subsequent social experience beyond the immediate family particularly at school and on the playground. Eventually the entire repertoire of behaviors and responses which has been internalized through largely unconscious processes is categorized by the child in conscious verbal ways. In other words, a little boy can tell you that he is a boy and what boys are like or for that matter what girls are like. So can a little girl, the main difference being that she can tell you sooner. It may well be that girls learn to speak earlier than boys do because they get spoken to earlier than boys do. That in turn may be because they are more responsive to that kind of input from their parents.

One additional comment must be made at this point and it has to do with the participation of the father in the nurture of the young child. There is a growing climate of opinion that his contribution has been less than it should be and that both he and the child have been impoverished as a result. Some persons are advocating that paternity leaves be granted by business and industry along with maternity leaves as a matter of public policy without undue financial sacrifice on the part of the parents. One benefit of such a policy would be to enrich the child rearing experience for both parents and children from the very outset. A second would be to modify or share some of the barriers to occupational continuity and advancement for women which are not placed in their husbands' way.

A related area in which there has been a shift in public opinion and medical practice has to do with the presence of the father at the time of the birth of the child. This includes appropriate training for the event for both mother and father. I was a part of the unfortunate generation when medical science was in process of transition so far as birthing practices are concerned, born thirty years too soon or too late. My birth took place in my parents' farmhouse in the days when that was still a family function. So far as I know my father was present and played a significant role, even if it was simply gathering towels and heating a kettle of water.

By the time my children were born, this function had been professionalized and sterilized. Our babies were born in a hospital under circumstances from which I was effectively excluded. It was apparently a matter which was none of my concern, something which affected only my wife and her doctor and the nurses. Only when they had completed their task was I informed of the results and permitted a brief peek through a glass window at these strange little creatures who would someday call me father. Perhaps this new generation of participating fathers will be better equipped psychologically than my generation which excluded fathers from their role in child rearing.

Christian Nurture

There is yet another language and its corresponding identity to be learned in the families of Christian parents; it is the language and identity of faith. Nor is its mastery totally separate from the process we have just described. It is rather that same process as seen from the perspective of Christian faith. That perspective provides not only a specific content but permeates the whole context of the socialization process and profoundly affects its texture and its goals.

The prototype for this kind of nurture is to be found in ancient Israel, where the faith was passed on from one generation to the next in the midst of daily living.

> And these words which I command you this day shall be upon your heart; and you shall teach them diligently to your children, and shall talk of them when you sit in your house, and when you walk by the way, and when you lie down, and when you rise. And you shall bind them as a sign upon your hand, and they shall be as frontlets between your eyes. And you shall write them on the doorposts of your house and on your gates. Deuteronomy 6:6-9.

Long before the advent of synagogue schools, the children were asking their parents, "What is the meaning of these stones?" and they would reply, "Once we were slaves in Egypt but God delivered us from bondage. He raised up Moses to be our leader and brought us out of Egypt, through the sea, over the desert, and to the mountain. There he made a covenant with us and made us his people. Then he led us through the wilderness for forty years and finally he brought us over the Jordan into this land which is now our home." What a tremendous recital of the history of this people! What a powerful lesson in history, or geography, or sociology, or theology! All this material was vital to the children's sense of identity. It told them where they came from, who their people were, and who they were. It helped them to locate themselves in terms of their social context, their moral obligation, their religious heritage and destiny.

We have already seen that the socialization process has to do with helping the growing person to establish and clarify his/her sense of identity. How does the perspective of Christian faith affect the texture of that identity? Earlier we noted that one of the meanings of the "image of God" in which we are created has to do with our capacity for relationship. We are made for fellowship with God and for fellowship with all other persons who are made in God's image. It is in these relationships that we experience both life's greatest joys and its greatest problems. Our relationships reflect both the agony and the ecstasy of our being. When we communicate with others, talk and listen, hear and understand, are heard and understood, love and are loved, we are most happy and most secure. When we cannot get through to others or they cannot reach us, when we are ignored or misunderstood, when we hate or are hated, we are most miserable and least certain of who we are.

The task of the family in Christian nurture is to help growing persons learn to communicate with each other, to hear and to be heard, to forgive and to be forgiven, to accept and to be accepted, to love and to be loved, in short, to belong and to feel secure in that belonging. That process, so common to our everyday life in families, is part of what it means to express the image of God in our personalities. A simpler way of expressing it is learning to say "we." It is in our "we" relationships that we exist. One cannot be a person all alone. This is, I believe, the profoundest theological meaning of family and one of the reasons that family images (brother, son, sister, daughter, mother, father, bride, groom) are among the images of the New Testament which illumine the nature of life together as persons of faith.

Two components of the "we" relationship are "you" and "I." It is in my interaction with you that I emerge. There is no such thing as personality apart from relationships. I emerge with all my powers of thinking, feeling, acting, hoping, and so forth in the context of my family. All of the uniquely personal powers of deciding, exploring, solving problems, persuading, competing, and the like are first learned in their most elemental, therefore profoundest, form in the family. Behind each word (and these represent only a small beginning) lies the drama of our being and our becoming. Written into the script of that drama is the view of life which is actually lived in the family; this is what provides the child with the lived experiences out of which grow the thought structures and the vocabulary by means of which all subsequent experiences are organized. What I have been trying to say has been expressed so much more effectively by someone else in these words,

Children Learn What They Live

If children live with criticism, they learn to condemn
If they live with hostility, they learn to fight
If they live with ridicule, they learn to be shy
If they live with shame, they learn to feel guilty
If they live with tolerance, they learn to be patient
If they live with encouragement, they learn to be confident
If they live with praise, they learn to appreciate
If they live with fairness, they learn a sense of justice
If they live with security, they learn to have faith
If they live with approval, they learn to like themselves
If they live with acceptance and friendship, they learn to find love in the world.

To say "I" is to make an affirmation. To say "me" is to make a self-appraisal, an evaluation. It is to look objectively at myself, to recognize both my strengths and my limitations. To do this we need the help of others. The problem in gaining true objectivity about ourselves is that we get mixed and unclear signals from others. Even those that are clear are filtered through our own defense systems to screen out what is most painful and threatening. Many a young person (and some older ones as well) keep asking such questions as, Am I a person of worth? Can I expect to be respected? maybe even to be loved? We get our earliest and emotionally most significant signals and answers to these questions in the family, of course. These are modified only through powerful reinforcement or painful experience in other life settings. Through genuine appreciation for growth and achievement as well as through loving discipline and nurture, the family builds up a true objectivity and an appropriate sense of worth in each of its members. It will only be possible for a child to grasp the meaning of "Jesus loves you" and "God forgives you" where love and forgiveness are part of the daily round of life.

We have already examined in the previous section the process by means of which the young child learns to say "she" and "he" and how gender identity is internalized into the way the little boy or girl says "I" and "me." Here we wish to stress only that Christian parents have a special responsibility to have each child grasp the sense of worth and dignity that inheres in both femininity and masculinity, for both alike and in relationship with each other are an expression of the image of God.

The other component of the "we" relationship is "you." "We" means "you and I." It takes the growing child a long time to give up the fondly held notion that mother is simply an extension of his own ego who exists solely for the purpose of satisfying his need to be fed, changed, cuddled, and rocked to sleep. Only later does he discover and acknowledge that she is a person in her own right with her own needs and preferences which he must learn to respect. It is not until late adolescence that these two organisms resolve their mutual dependence with the psychological snipping of the umbilical cord and the apron strings.

When the infant leaves the nursery and enters the larger world of siblings and playmates, he makes an exciting but painful discovery when he encounters others. As he moves around, he comes into contact with other warm bodies which he pushes, hugs, kicks, kisses, and otherwise generally explores with all the empirical tools at his disposal. These bodies push, hug, kick, kiss, and generally explore his body in return. As these budding young behavioral scientists mill around, they soon discover that some behavior elicits hugs and kisses while other behavior provokes pushes and kicks. In ways like these they become socially aware and socially responsive. Becoming socially responsive and responsible involves something of a disciplined effort in which parental or adult supervision and direction are needed. As children grow older, they learn that there are certain expectations they must fulfill in order to live in harmony with others. They learn what it is to make mistakes, to forget, perhaps even to do deliberate damage to one another, and eventually to seek or offer forgiveness and be reconciled.

It is also in the family as we have seen that the gift of speech is cultivated. While the capacity for speech is given, a particular language must always be learned. What joy attends a baby's first words! What powerful reinforcement undergirds and reinforces a baby's initial attempts at communication and persuades the baby to translate those incomprehensible grunts into articulate sounds! The capacity to speak is one of the most profound and wonderful abilities we have as persons. To be sure, the schools help us to cultivate that ability, to develop and express our thoughts clearly. However, long before the schools begin their work, the basic structure of our thought and speech patterns on which they build is formed by the family. The same is true of the church school. While our children develop their specifically Christian vocabulary and expand and modify their theological concepts through the church school, the success of that effort will depend to a large extent on what has happened and what is happening in our homes.

The church expresses itself as a community of faith through its use of a common language; the source of its language is the Bible. James Gustafson has said, "Belonging to the Christian community means knowing its common language. The church is a community because communication within it occurs through common verbal symbols."[21] The church uses this common language in most or all of its varied activities: worship, proclamation, pastoral care, instruction, fellowship, baptism, the Lord's Supper, evangelism, administration, and service. Language plays a more central role in some of these activities than in others; it is one of the means, though not the sole one, of communication within the community and between the community and those outside it. Christian nurture is concerned with teaching this common language to all persons who become members of this community. Doctrinal instruction is a major part of this teaching but the whole task is larger than formal instruction in the intellectual content of the Christian faith.

There are many occasions for introducing children to the great words and concepts of the Christian gospel in the course of family living. Children raise many questions and many of these are religious questions. Their questionings are prompted by conversations they hear, books they read, things they see, crises they experience. It is a common experience for parents, even for theologically trained ones, to be hard pressed to give a reasonable account of their faith in response to their children's sincere curiosity. They need first of all to have a mature understanding of it themselves, both experientially and cognitively. In addition they must be able to interpret it on the child's level in terms of the specific questions the child is raising at the time.

Learning the language of faith is an important part of learning to participate in the worship of the Christian community. Reuel Howe states that many persons find it difficult or even impossible to worship because certain human experiences have been missing in their lives. The experiences of love and trust are "indispensable preconditions for worship."[22] Howe believes that the love of the parent for the child, though it is limited and partial, is used of God to prepare the child for responding to his love. Similarly, trust is awakened in the early months of the child's existence through its dependent status and the ministrations of the persons (primarily the mother and father) with whom the child is in relationship. The capacity for trusting God is profoundly conditioned by this early experience in the family.

Another way in which the family can prepare the growing child for meaningful participation in the worshiping community is through worship in the home. The habits of worship, the discipline of prayer, the familiarity with religious language and ritual, the learning of songs and hymns, and the memorization of the Scriptures carry over into the worship of the congregation. Where the congregation provides for a family worship service, the family by its presence and active participation initiates the child into meaningful participation in the worshiping life of the church.

The Family as Launching Center

The final consideration we wish to examine in this section is that the experience of genuine community in the Christian family and in the congregation prepares the growing person for meaningful participation in the community at large. The natural communities are the sphere into which the person is called to live the life of faith. The church and the family together prepare the person for a Christian vocation. While vocation is a broader concept than daily work, it does comprehend the latter within it. It should be noted that most persons discharge their Christian vocation in the world primarily, though not exclusively, in and through their occupation. The way in which Christian persons discharge their Christian vocation through their work sheds light also on the person's total vocation in the world as well. Paul Minear defines vocation as "a person's conception of the central purpose of his life. He adopts this purpose consciously and voluntarily, and seeks to realize it through whatever channels may be provided by successive situations."[23]

Christian persons recognize that the life of faith extends beyond the community of faith; the life of love for the neighbor carries one out into the world where the neighbor lives and works. For this reason the Christian makes no distinction between secular tasks and participation in God's work except as the secular tasks may interfere in that work; in that case the secular tasks must be rejected as inappropriate to one's Christian calling.

How does the family prepare the growing person for meaningful involvement in the world of work? First, it should be recognized that the family is not the only agency which participates in that preparation. The church also has a responsibility to interpret the human situation and one's Christian vocation within it as well as to lead the person to an active acceptance of that responsibility in the world.

The Christian family may contribute in a number of ways to the interpretation of the world of work from a Christian perspective. Most important of all is the fact that the family is itself a community of shared responsibilities in which each one is called upon to assume part of the common task. The technical, social, and moral responsibilities later to be encountered on the job are first encountered in the family. To be sure, the particular technical skills of the job in our time are not learned in the family. However, the demand for responsible behavior with reference to things, to persons, and to God is essentially the same wherever it is encountered and in whatever particular form.

The great lessons of interdependence and responsibility learned in the family have a transfer value to all subsequent experiences of community. In the Christian family, these lessons may be invested with religious meaning with the result that the person's job may also come to be viewed from a religious point of view. This is done, in part, through the chance comments that pass between parents and children in the course of working and living together. Informal conversation about their experiences in the world of work when they return to the home is one vehicle of communicating parental attitudes toward work; it may become the medium of the Christian interpretation of vocation. The family is in a unique position to foster ideals, integrity, duty, cooperation, and service which profoundly affect the way in which persons view their vocation and carry out their daily work.

Burgess and Locke devoted a chapter in their book, *The Family: From Institution to Companionship*, to the influence of the family upon children in preparing them for their roles in the wider society.[24] They note that as children grow into contact with other communities in their environment, the values and patterns of the family may well come into conflict with those outside. A sorting out process occurs in which family established roles are consolidated, modified, or rejected. If children have been encouraged through their developing years to assume personal responsibility, if their families have provided them with a secure home base from which to venture forth and to which to return, if their parents do not feel threatened by their increasing emotional and physical independence, the family will have served them well as a launching center.

Conclusion

The progression of thought in the first three chapters has moved from a theology of sexuality through a theology of marriage to a theology of the family. The issue of fecundity is yet a third area of the sexual revolution (along with gender identity/roles and sexual morality); it underlies the current debate in all areas, not only contraception and abortion, but touches vitally the questions of the meaning of marriage and of the sex roles as well as of the very meaning of sexuality itself. We have explored the growing tendency to divorce sex from procreation and to see its meaning primarily in terms of recreation. We have examined the issue of how the respective roles of females and males in the reproductive process affect their larger social roles.

Childbearing and child rearing are seen by some sexual revolutionaries as impediments to women finding full equality with men in the marketplace. Without equal opportunity and reward in employment, it is said, women will not achieve full economic, social, and political equality. This in turn has caused some persons to raise the question of how worth is to be measured. Are we to measure it only or even primarily in terms of money? Are the bearing and rearing of children not of equal social value with other tasks carried out outside the home? Would paying money for these tasks elevate their dignity and status?

Finally we looked at the role of the family in the socialization of the young child and from a Christian perspective for the Christian nurture of the young child. Both of these processes, so similar in many ways, involve the development of a sense of identity and the learning of a language. In one case, it involves learning the mother tongue; in the other, it is a matter of learning the language of faith.

Learning a language is a highly complex task; it is not only an intellectual skill but one that involves the whole psychosomatic organism in its total environment. This complex task has fallen to our families long before the schools take on its further elaboration and refinement. It is a significant contribution which our families have made to all of us and one whose dignity and importance are not enhanced by professionalizing it. Nor is it cheapened in any way by considering it to be part of life rather than a way of making a living.

Developing an identity as a person, male or female, and developing the identity of a child of God are likewise profound contributions of the family to growing boys and girls. For families to fulfill these responsibilities, there must be an openness to the rich resources of God's grace. It is not the human perfection of the parents but the presence of God in family living which provides the nutrients for the growing of Christian persons. The family, to be sure, depends on many outside resources including the public school and the church school to carry out its role. Moreover, the effectiveness of families as we know them often leaves much to be desired. However, no satisfactory substitute for this primary community of love and affection has been designed for the meeting of our deepest human needs and for the socialization process at its earliest and deepest levels.

4
Forth from the Garden: The Family in Transition

Then the Lord God said,
"Behold,
the man has become like one of us,
knowing good and evil;
and now,
lest he put forth his hand and take also
of the tree of life,
and eat,
and live forever"—
therefore the Lord God sent him forth
from the garden of Eden,
to till the ground
from which he was taken.
Genesis 3:22-23.

You may have heard the wisecrack about Adam and Eve as they left the garden of Eden. Adam turned to Eve and said, "My dear, our family is about to enter into a period of transition." It is true that the changes in human relationships brought about by the fall were devastating to all parties concerned. Adam scapegoated his wife; one of his sons murdered his brother and from there on it was bad news all down the line. Change and disruption have been characteristic of human existence all through recorded history. Nonetheless the rapidity of social change which has taken place in the middle of the twentieth century is without precedent.

In the first three chapters we have explored some of the changes in marriage and family living which are taking place as the direct result of the determined efforts of the sexual revolutionaries. In their analysis of the situation, society is in bondage and must be liberated from its oppression. They speak of "liberation" with respect to three aspects of sexuality, marriage, and the family: (a) "liberation" from gender role/identity stereotypes and the rigid patterns of the patriarchal family; (b) "liberation" from a "repressive" sexual ethic and the "unnatural" confines of monogamous marriage; and (c) "liberation" from the "tyranny" of the biological family, that is, from bearing and rearing children.

The revolution is fueled by powerful ideologies based on the values of individualism and self-realization. In addition there are underlying scientific and technological developments which create a supportive climate in which the winds of change may blow more freely.

Up to this point we have viewed the family as the object of social and ideological forces operating upon it. However, now the angle of vision with regard to "liberation" shifts. From this point on we view the family as subject, drawing on its resources to confront and challenge alien social and ideological forces and to create an environment in which its self-chosen values, patterns, and goals are dominant.

In this chapter we review a major project devoted to testing this proposition, National Case Studies of the Family Unit in Changing Societies, a project of the Office of Family Education of the World Council of Churches. The assumption underlying the project is well stated in a brochure introducing the program to Australian families by Dr. Cliff Wright, one of its designers, as follows:

> Families need not be victims, always acted upon by outside forces. They need not wait for others to tell them what to do, what to think, what to buy, what value systems to uphold, what goals for living to accept. They can become more self-reliant, more liberated, less other-directed. They can stand more on their own feet, overcome fatalistic attitudes, become initiating centers for needed change, subjects rather than objects.

Before reviewing the project and its findings, we will summarize the literature on the issue of how social change affecting the family comes about. What evidence, if any, is there that families can "become initiating centers for needed change" and exert an influence on their environment? Can families say "no" to social, political, economic, and ideological forces which sweep them up in their powerful forward movement? Can they retard the momentum of these forces and modify their impact? Can they create and launch counterforces which will serve to vitiate the power and appeal of current trends and provide attractive alternatives based on different assumptions and values? These are critical questions as Christians in families search together for a strategy to enable them to come to terms with their life in the world today.

Without doubt, the social environment within which

the family lives shapes its values, its patterns of interaction, its style of life. Some sociologists have concluded that in the traffic between the family and the larger society, the traffic is more of a one-way street from the wider environment to the family shaping it into its mold. If this is the case, it is clear that no single family by itself alone will be able to withstand those shaping influences. What must happen is that there must be developed a counterculture, a social environment within which our families can exist, an alliance of Christian families committed to values different from those of the dominant culture around them.

Changing Family Forms and Functions

Where did the family as we know it come from? What forms did family life take in antiquity? Prior to the development of modern sociology and cross-cultural anthropological studies of families in primitive societies, nineteenth century scholars speculated about the shape and origin of the earliest human families. Three models have been proposed: sexual promiscuity, matriarchy, and patriarchy. In light of the fact that there is no prehistorical literary documentation, all such theories remain speculative. Professor Bernard I. Murstein of Connecticut College, who devoted nearly a decade to researching the history of love, sex, and marriage through the ages before publishing his monumental work under that title in 1974, concludes that "the truth of the matter is that we do not know with even a modest degree of certitude how the family actually got started."[1]

Some scholars like H. J. S. Maine in 1861 held that patriarchy was the earliest known form of family life.[2] Others like Friedrich Engels[3] argued, however, that since patriarchy was so closely linked with private property, it must have been preceded by a matriarchal period before the appearance of private property. It was at that time, he alleged, that men began their exploitation and subjugation of women in order to gain control of property and to be able to pass it on to their sons. Monogamy was seen in the same light, as a necessity in order to ensure that their property was inherited only by their legitimate offspring and not by the children of their wives sired by other males. In Engels' theory, matriarchy had in turn been preceded by a period of sexual promiscuity in which there was no stable family system.

Such speculation, as Christopher Lasch has pointed out, owed a great deal to two other phenomena of those times, (a) Darwin's theory of evolution and (b) the political philosophy of socialism. By studying the historical development of family systems in the light of evolutionary principles, the analysis, it was believed, could be projected backward through time into antiquity before there were historical records available. Secondly, the strong ideological flavor of analyses like Engels' was so obvious that Max Weber referred to the matriarchal theory as the "socialistic theory of the family."4 If the family is seen as being tied to a particular stage in the economic evolution of society, the family will either disappear or be radically altered as the social revolution takes place sweeping all social and economic institutions before it.

While it cannot be proved or disproved that patriarchy was the earliest form of family life, it can certainly be said that it has dominated civilization in most societies of which there is historical record. This is especially true of the biblical period as recorded both in the Old Testament and even in the New. It may be because there were no other family patterns known to Paul that he lent his efforts to modifying and softening the harsher features of patriarchy rather than to proposing an alternative model. ("Husbands, love your wives, as Christ loved the church.... Fathers, do not provoke your children to anger, but bring them up in the discipline and instruction of the Lord.... Masters, ... forbear threatening [your slaves], knowing that he who is both their Master and yours is in heaven, and that there is no partiality with him" (Ephesians 5:25; 6:4, 9).

Modern sociology has shown little interest in speculation about the origins and original patterns of family life but has concentrated instead on empirical descriptions of present and emerging family structures. In 1945 Ernest W. Burgess and Harvey J. Locke argued that the patriarchal family (which they identified as the closest approximation to the institutional type of family) was giving way in American society to a new type labeled by them as the companionship family. They stated that "the basic thesis of this book is that the family in historical times has been in transition from an institution with family behavior controlled by the mores, public opinion and law to a companionship with family behavior arising from the mutual affection and consensus of its members."[5]

The two typologies were contrasted by such categories as patriarchal vs. democratic, formal vs. informal, structural vs. relational, fixed roles vs. flexible roles, emphasis on duty and responsibility vs. emphasis on affection and intimacy. The primary function of the companionship family is to provide an intimate interpersonal climate. The marks of such a family are the giving and receiving of affection, the equality of husband and wife, participation by all in all decisions, the personality development of each member as a major objective, the freedom for each member to express himself/herself, and the expectation that the greatest happiness in life is to be found in the family.

Talcott Parsons has described the American family

as an "open, multi-lineal, conjugal system."[6] This description is most characteristic of the urban middle-class American family which seems to be the dominant pattern of American families. The conjugal family, or the nuclear family as it is sometimes called, is at the heart of the structure; it is relatively isolated from other families in this same system. Conjugal or nuclear families live in their own house or apartment; their place of residence may be hundreds of miles away from close family relatives. They make their own decisions about lifestyle (money, travel, education, religion, politics). They are financially independent. Neither the male nor the female need secure parental permission to marry if they are of legal age. The honeymoon symbolizes the break with parents and family. The marriage is built on an agreement between two persons based on romantic love, not an arrangement between two families based on more practical considerations. The jokes about in-laws are a subtle or not so subtle defense system to guard the privacy and the structural isolation of the married couple.

While this family system fits American culture well and is responsive to its values, it is also extremely vulnerable to the pressures and influences of the larger society which are expressed through television and the mass media, changing mores and peer group standards apart from the larger family. Parsons states that the structural isolation of today's nuclear family, determined by the patterns and ideals of contemporary culture and admirably suited to it, "underlies most of its peculiar functional and dynamic problems."[7]

The nuclear family is less and less surrounded and influenced by the values of the extended family of parents, brothers, sisters, aunts, uncles, cousins, and grandparents on both sides. It is tied more and more into the larger society and influenced by its values, trends, and resources. The nuclear family emphasizes love and affection (as over against duty and responsibility); the relative independence of the new family unit; freedom of choice in mate selection with less attention given to similarity of background; equality of husband and wife and even limited interchangeability of roles; participation by all, including children, in family decisions; and freedom for each person to express himself/herself and to develop his/her personality and gifts to the fullest extent possible.

Since this is such a great system, why doesn't it work? Parsons observes that the husband-wife relationship is the "main structural keystone"[8] of this family system. This places a heavier burden on the affectional bond between the spouses than it did in those family systems where the emotional relationships of the family members were more diffuse. Both affection and tension were scattered throughout the larger family network. The wife, for example, could work through some of the tensions she was experiencing in her relationship with her husband by talking it out with her mother, her sister, her brother, her grandmother, or any one of several persons intimately related to her. The influence, or pressure, if you will, of that larger kinship group was brought to bear upon the quarreling spouses to resolve their problems or, if that was impossible, at least to maintain the appearance of unity so as not to embarrass the larger family.

Since the conjugal family depends more heavily on that husband-wife bond for its stability than does the extended family, it becomes by that very fact more fragile and vulnerable to disruption when that bond is weakened. In other words, two forces have conspired to weaken and disrupt the family system. The first is the weakening of the support structure which surrounds or undergirds the nuclear family as extended family ties are diminished both through changing social values and through geographical scattering as families become more mobile. The second is the greater pressures on the husband and wife of modern family living which make intimacy more difficult even as it becomes more important.

Another way of saying this is to think of the husband-wife relationship as a bridge. What modern society has done is to remove the supporting pillars of the extended family from under the bridge leaving only the pillars of the husband and the wife. The bridge has therefore been weakened at the same time that heavier traffic is moving over it. Small wonder that the bridge of marriage collapses as frequently as it does!

Parsons' concept of the relative structural isolation of the nuclear family has been challenged recently by Eugene Litwack and Melvin Seeman.[9] They emphasize the significance of the network of relationships between the nuclear couple and their children on the one hand and the extended kinship group of which they are a part on the other. Parsons acknowledges that these ties are not broken; he had never intended to imply that. However, he continues to insist that they are lessening in their crucial significance. Extended families are not residential or economic units either as producers or consumers as you have for example in the Hutterite communities. Communication among family members is sporadic and highly selective, that is, visiting, common activities, communication by phone or letter. The relatives are "a resource which may selectively be taken advantage of within considerable limits," a "reserve of expectations of solidarity and willingness to implement them which can be mobilized in case of need."[10] Economic independence among adult brothers and sisters, adult children, and parents of adult children is assumed. This is to be seen, for example, in a statement commonly heard from older parents, "I don't want to be a burden on my children." In earlier years, the responsibility of persons for their aging parents including making a home for them in their family circle was not spoken of as a burden.

At the same time, in the event of a crisis or severe need, the extended family does represent a backup system to a limited degree. In really severe cases, a family needing help may appeal to cousins, aunts, and uncles. Examples might include the death of both parents of small children in an accident or an aged penniless adult without children provided he lost his money in the stock market crash and didn't simply convert it into liquid assets and drink it up. While the network is there, the tendency is to value independence from it except in dire circumstances and to function for all practical purposes as though it did not exist.

The word "multi-lineal" in Parsons' definition simply means that many different family lines flow together into the new conjugal family unit. This is obviously the case in any marriage within any marriage system. However, the thing that is worthy of note is that in the traditional extended family system the family lines which flowed together into a new marriage tended to have a great deal in common by way of religious, cultural, ethnic, and social background. Today, there is considerable diversity of background between the marrying partners. This is what is meant by the word "open" in the definition; it simply refers to the assumption that everyone is theoretically free to marry whomever she/he wishes to marry.

It is this characteristic that is being increasingly underscored in new patterns of marriage. The independence of the new marital unit from the old is enhanced by the element of free choice in the selection of the marriage partner. Even in systems where marriages were not arranged, the values and preferences of the extended family tended to enter strongly in informal ways into the selection of a mate. This is, of course, the drama underlying *Fiddler on the Roof* in which there is a direct challenge to Tevye's parental authority in determining whom his daughters will marry. By the time the third daughter marries, differences in cultural and religious backgrounds are totally ignored. Furthermore, romantic considerations in mate selection take precedence over prudential ones; in other words, the heart wins out over the head.

Undeniably, the institution of the American family has undergone significant changes over the past several centuries as the sociocultural environment in which it exists has been modified. These changes and their underlying causes have been well documented by a number of social scientists, notably by Burgess and Locke. The consensus is that traditional functions of the family such as the economic, protective, recreational, educational, and religious functions, while not entirely eliminated and transferred to other agencies, have been significantly modified.

In 1955, a study by W. F. Ogburn and M. F. Nimkoff, *Technology and the Changing Family,* set forth the thesis that of all the factors contributing to changes in the family, scientific discoveries and technological advances are among the most significant. To establish their theory they polled a panel of 18 responsible observers of the family for their opinion as to what constituted the outstanding changes in the family in recent times. A total of 63 changes were named indicating that the family had undergone extensive modification. On the other hand, a consensus emerged on what constituted the basic changes in family life. Three of them had to do with the formation and disruption of the family: romance as the basic consideration for marriage, earlier marriages, and divorce. A second cluster of changes had to do with the interrelationships of various family members: husband/father, wife/mother, children/siblings. This analysis dealt with working wives, distribution of authority, and the emphasis on the child. The remaining two changes concerned the decreasing size of families and the shift in traditional functions of the family.

The conclusion of the study was that while in the course of adaptation the family has lost many of its functions, these things remain and assume a correspondingly greater importance, "the personality functions dealing with companionship, affection and education."[12] This is also the judgment of anthropologist Ralph Linton,[13] who insists that only the family can offer the surest guarantee of meeting the most basic human needs which are the need for love, acceptance, and affection. In his view, this alone ensures that the family as a social organism will survive even though its functions are diminished and its forms change. No satisfactory substitute for child rearing and the socialization of the young has been devised, the conspicuous failures of the family notwithstanding.

Theories of Social Change

Sociologist Richard R. Clayton has written an excellent summary of four major theories of social change which have been applied to analyses of families in transition. The first of these is the *evolutionary* theory which holds that "all societies move from a simple to a more complex state."[14] An example of this kind of analysis would be that of Friedrich Engels discussed earlier. Engels along with other socialist theorists looked forward to a time when the patriarchal family would be swept away along with capitalism and private property of which it was a necessary correlate. A more complex system of male-female relationships would evolve in its place reflecting the new socioeconomic order of socialism. The main feature of this order would be sexual freedom in which a woman would no longer be considered as the exclusive sexual property of a man. The experiments in alternate intimate lifestyles described in a previous chapter would be viewed in this analysis as harbingers of the new social order. However, David and Vera Mace describe them as vestigial remnants of an earlier era which modern society has left behind in its evolutionary development toward the companionship family.

Whether or not one agrees with the evolutionary theory of social change, we can certainly agree that moving from monogamy to group marriage is a movement in the direction of simple to complex. The management of such a web of human relationships is so complex that such efforts are doomed to a short existence. The most celebrated of such attempts is the Oneida Community of upstate New York, which lasted for about thirty years before it disintegrated.[15] It is also very interesting to follow the changes in the respective family codes of Russia (1918, 1936, and 1944) in which there are successive deliberate changes in marriage and divorce laws and policies and practices regarding childbearing which reflect not a forward moving evolutionary development but a return to more traditional concepts of marriage and the family.[16]

A second theory of the process of social change is the *developmental* theory, characterized by Gerald R. Leslie as the *cyclical* theory.[17] Carle Zimmerman is cited by Clayton and Leslie as a representative of this theory as outlined in his monumental study in 1949, *The Family of Tomorrow: The Cultural Crisis and the Way Out.* According to this theory, both individuals and institutions go through the various stages of development which characterize the individual life cycle from infancy to maturity followed by a period of decline and ultimately death. The developmental theory with respect to the family is fairly pessimistic and so was Zimmerman so far as the American family in the latter part of the twentieth century is concerned. Certainly the changes in sexual values and practices and their disintegrating impact on marital and familial stability would seem to be adequate documentation for Zimmerman's prognosis if not for his theory. But there is also a sense in which his theory is an optimistic one for he sees the possibility of reversing or at least delaying the decline of the family. What is called for is a vigorous program on the part of the government and the church to restore the family to its rightful place of influence and status in society.

A third theory of social change is called *functional* by Clayton and *progressivist* by Leslie.[18] This theory measures social change by observing the changes in functions that occur in any given social unit such as the family over a period of time. Ogburn and Nimkoff's study, *Technology and the Changing Family* (1955), is a good example of this theory.[19] These shifts in family functions (economic, educational, religious, recreational, protective, status-conferring, and affectional) are the result of larger social forces in the family's environment. These forces include industrialization, urbanization, and technology with their increasingly complex social and economic structures. In Clayton's view, the family is seen as the passive subject being shaped into the mold of these powerful forces. "For Ogburn the family is the recipient of change, almost always the dependent variable, while Zimmerman saw the family system as the locus and instigator of change."[20]

Clayton and Leslie each identify an additional theory though there seems to be no correlation between the two. Leslie refers to a *structure-function* theory whose best known exponent is Talcott Parsons, whose model of the relative structural isolation of the nuclear family we have already traced. Its focus is on the interaction and integration between the family and other institutions with special reference to the world of work.[21] When this is the focus, the changes in family function are not viewed as diminishing or weakening but as creative adaptation to its changing environment.

The family has, in this view, adapted amazingly well to the modern industrial situation. When production was primarily a total family operation such as you had with the family farm, the family took on the shape of the extended kinship group. When production moved out of the bosom of the family into the factories and firms, the family adapted by shrinking its size to the nuclear unit, became urbanized and mobile. This has caused some observers such as Nimkoff and Middleton to come to conclusions quite the opposite of the evolutionary theory of movement from the simple to the complex. They stated that

> the modern industrial society, with its small independent family, is then like the simpler hunting and gathering society and, in part, apparently for some of the same reasons, namely, limited need for family labor and physical mobility. The hunter is mobile because he pursues the game: the industrial worker, the job.[22]

Clayton's fourth theory is the *tension management* model. The tension is created by the opposing forces in any society, some of which advocate change while others seek to control and restrict those forces to preserve existing values and patterns. This tension is clearly evident in the prochange forces of the sexual revolution and in the reactions they have evoked on the part of their opponents, notably the self-styled Moral Majority. This makes it necessary for the family to take a stand and resolve the issues at stake according to its own best insights and requirements. The process by which it comes to terms with these conflicting forces is called tension management.[23]

The basic issue in which we are interested in all these theories of social change is the role of the family as active or passive, as initiator of change or passive subject. Clayton concludes,

> Growing out of all these studies of the changing family has come a consensus, at least of sorts. For example, there is fairly widespread agreement that the family as a unit within a community and as a system within society is more a recipient than an initiator of social change. There is also consensus that four interlocking causal variables in family change are industrialization, urbanization, societal complexity, and modernization.[24]

There are, as we have seen, some spokesmen for another point of view including Talcott Parsons, who is quoted as saying, "I believe profoundly in the importance of the family system, and I furthermore don't think it always follows, but at times it leads, social change."[25] The testimony of Meyer Nimkoff, who collaborated with William Ogburn in the 1955 study, *Technology and the Changing Family*, is also significant in this regard:

> Even though technological and other economic factors may be the prime movers (accounting for more variation in social systems than do ideological factors), still the family is an independent as well as a dependent variable and may exert significant influence on the social process.[26]

With respect to ideological factors (as over against scientific and technological forces) at work in the processes of social change, J. Richard Udry in his book, *The Social Context of Marriage*, has identified four belief systems that are embedded in various ways in the American value system which affect the values of the family, undergirding the family structure in similar ways that a foundation undergirds a house.

The first of these is the *Christian tradition* which has had an effect on shaping Western social thought, institutions, and practices, even for those who are not practicing Christians. For example, the celebration of marriage has traditionally been viewed as a basically religious event. The Western view of marriage is that it is a monogamous and permanent relationship. For a long time adultery was seen by the state as the only legitimate ground for divorce. Even though the divorce rate has been increasing at an alarming rate, it is still viewed as an unfortunate tragedy rather than as an occasion for celebration. In this is to be seen the residual view that marriage should be monogamous and permanent. The traditional Christian view also affirms having children as a good thing. Premarital and extramarital sex (fornication and adultery) are prohibited.

A second belief system embedded in American values is *democratic equalitarianism.*

> The doctrine of the equality of all men and the right of individuals to participate in the decisions affecting their fate began as a political creed, but has selectively been diffused into other social relationships.... Americans are now in a position of combining traditions which legitimize the authority of men over women and adults over children with a democratic-equalitarian attitude which undercuts this formerly legitimate authority and emphasizes equality of the sexes and the rights of children to be spared from arbitrary authority.[27]

There is in our society a powerful tension between the newly emerging trend which emphasizes the equal rights of all to be heard and considered on the one hand versus the residual traditional attitude of male authority over women and of adult authority over children.

The Equal Rights Amendment, which at the time of this writing has not finally cleared the needed two-thirds of the state legislatures in the U.S., has stirred up a great deal of controversy among both men and women. It is a brief and simple statement which on the face of it should not be controversial. "Equality of rights under the law shall not be denied or abridged by the United States or by any State on account of sex." It is controversial because it is calling into question and sweeping aside many of the old laws and practices which governed male-female relationships in the political, legal, and economic spheres of life. Opponents of the amendment have played up the uncertainty of the nature and extent of the changes it will bring knowing that many people are willing to tolerate a less than satisfactory system because the old and the known represent a measure of security and stability in spite of their deficiencies.

A third belief system which is affecting the foundations of marriage and the family is *individualism,* a philosophy that asserts that the individual is more important than the group:

> The goals of the individual are given preference and his well-being and happiness are the criteria for social and individual decisions. It is not the duty of the individual to sacrifice his happiness for the well-being of other people. The individual personality is honored and the development of its potential is a worthy goal.[28]

Individualism has made its impact on such issues as grounds for divorce, grounds for abortion, marriage folkways, etc.

The fourth belief system identified by Udry is *secularism.* "A secular society is one in which there is a generalized willingness to change patterns and traditional beliefs as contrasted to a sacred society in which people are reluctant and resistant to social change of any kind."[29] The evidence of our living in a secular society is to be seen in that traditional Christian concepts concerning marriage and the family are being significantly eroded in favor of new concepts, values, and practices. Illustrations are to be found in changing age and sex roles, the growing acceptance of divorce and re-marriage in society generally and even in the church, the growing acceptance of contraception and family planning, liberal abortion laws, and a growing acceptance of alternative lifestyles.

All this provides us with awesome and persuasive evidence that families are passive victims of overwhelmingly powerful technological, industrial, economic, social, political, and ideological forces. In light of these realities, it is all the more striking that a group of family life educators representing Christian churches around the world should design a project based on the conviction that families can take control of their destiny and determine what kind of world they are going to live in. The popular name by which this project came to be known was Family Power for Social Change.

Family Power for Social Change

Eighty kilometers south of Mexico City there is an oasis with a commanding view of Mount Popocatepetl called Oaxtepec. Many years ago it was one of Montezuma's favorite health spas. Oaxtepec was the site of a family assembly convened in January, 1980, by the Office of Family Education of the World Council of Churches— the first of a number of major events focusing on family life issues to be held in 1980:

(a) the National Conference on the Family in Thailand, April, 1980, sponsored by the Church of Christ in Thailand;

(b) the World Congress on Family Policy in Milan, June, 1980, sponsored by the International Family Studies Center;

(c) the conference on the theme "The Child and the Family: Today and Tomorrow," in Mexico City, July, 1980, sponsored by the International Federation for Parent Education;

(d) the Bishops' Synod on the Family in Rome in the autumn of 1980 sponsored by the Vatican;

(e) the White House Conferences on the Family in late 1980 convened by the president of the United States.

The Family Power for Social Change Project, more formally called "National Case Studies of the Family Unit in Changing Societies," was a three-year project, 1976-79. Representatives of the 47 family groups in 23 countries together with family life specialists from these countries assembled to reflect on what had been learned. It was a colorful parade as the delegates, dressed in the traditional costumes of their respective cultures, came to the front to place their flags on the map of the world prepared by their Mexican hosts. In spite of the wide-ranging differences in culture, language, and tradition, the exchange of experiences and ideas was for the most part harmonious. There was, however, a clash of ideologies with respect to the process of change, though not in broad principle as to where that change should lead, that is, to peace in the world and social justice for all.

The assembly was convened in a veritable paradise, a retreat, recreation, and study center with modern equipment and facilities owned and operated by the government of Mexico. Just outside the well guarded gates of the campus, however, was the evidence of the poverty in which many of the people of Mexico actually live. This was an appropriate symbol of the project; the project groups represented the whole spectrum of the world's socioeconomic order. They ranged from the Finma group consisting primarily of professors at the University of Helsinki to some illiterate Mexican Indian women whose major preoccupation was how to obtain a safe and adequate supply of drinking water, from the economically secure European and North American groups to the group in North Sumatra whose concern had to do with elemental human needs such as food and health care.

Several Mexican Indian women from the Tarango group were present and happy to be included in the fellowship and discussion of the week. One of them was holding a tiny baby. When I asked her the baby's name, she replied beaming with pride and joy, "Jésus"; his name is Jesus. What a powerful symbol of hope in the face of what from a human point of view often seems hopeless!

The Family Power for Social Change Project emerged out of a meeting in Malta in 1973 which had been called to advise the Office of Family Education concerning future directions for its programs. The group took note of the wide range of "family structures, sex roles, educational patterns, and cultural and ideological value systems" of Christian families around the world. They questioned whether "traditional ministries to families were being outrun by deeper social changes and therefore were in danger of becoming irrelevant."

As a result of these observations and questions the Malta consultants proposed a new direction for family life ministries which tended in the past to focus on personal development and interpersonal relationships. This new direction called for families to confront their world, to challenge the assumptions on which many social changes are based, and to initiate efforts to challenge and direct social change in ways that enhance the well-being of the family. The term "family power" was "an attempt to highlight the fact that within the family there is a dynamism which if developed and released could be a powerful agent for change. The family need not be a victim always acted upon and subject to powers beyond its control."[30]

A program was designed which called for clusters of family groups in various countries around the world to meet regularly over a period of time in order to reflect on their situation, initiate some action in relation to it, and evaluate the results. Each primary group had an enabler and a backup system which consisted of key persons for various geographic regions as well as the Office of Family Education. Six working papers for the family groups were published in English, French, Spanish, and German. The resources of the Office of Family Education were made available to the project groups including consultations, correspondence, visits to some of the groups, and a communication network by means of which each group was informed about what was happening in other groups around the world. The very existence of this network was a source of encouragement and inspiration which significantly enhanced the efforts of the local groups.

A major feature of the design was for persons to tell their family stories from as far back as memory could serve. In this way the groups became aware of changes that had taken place in the past and were even now taking place and could seize the initiative in deciding on the direction of social change. Through this process of "family action/reflection research," these families were made keenly aware of changes which were profoundly affecting their family values and the very shape of their family life. In some cases they faced the opposite problem, that is, massive resistance to change which would be desirable. Family groups throughout the project noted with concern changing cultural values, marriage practices, methods of child rearing, male/female roles, and sexual values and practices.

One of the deep concerns which emerged in the traditional societies of Asia and Africa was the threat to the existence of the extended family posed by an increasingly industrialized society. The extended kinship family has provided a sense of identity, belonging, and stability for its members. There is great anxiety that the smaller nuclear family with its emphasis on mobility and individualism will not be able to provide these valued resources. Certainly the experience of family groups in the industrialized world is not a very reassuring harbinger of things to come.

Several groups in Australia, Canada, England, and New Zealand, where the nuclear family has become the basic pattern, expressed their own deep concerns about the inadequacies of that family pattern. The Waverly Cluster in Victoria, Australia, gathered around a simple issue, the quantity of garbage carried out by a family each week. The concern broadened and spread through the other families to include such things as plastics, packaging, herbicides for weed control, food and nutrition, vegetable growing, self-sufficiency, consumerism, and energy conservation. Eventually they began to question the wastefulness (in terms of both material and human resources) of nuclear family living and explored the option of cluster housing on common land. They decided to share washing machines, cars, and implements as well as companionship, child care, counseling, skills, and crafts. In their final evaluation they made this statement:

> The group sees the cluster style experience such as it had as an important instrument of social change. It is an intensely human group in the midst of great inhuman institutions. It is a community based on social values rather than on commercial or power-seeking or success oriented values. The cluster can provide the means for ordinary people to recover control over their lives and live by the values they hold dear rather than the externally imposed values of some institution, authority, government, or corporation concerned mainly with status, power, or profit. The cluster is a step towards a self-regulating society where the whole community deals with its own tensions, conflicts, and behavioral problems instead of handing these over to "experts" or outside authorities to resolve. The cluster can encourage its members to take a stand against the ever-increasing acquisitiveness of our society.

By agreeing to share resources, it is possible to curb the desire to accumulate wealth and possessions and encourage each other to simplify life styles.

The group's enabler, Barry Mitchell, added a footnote to the above report which had been prepared by a member of the group as follows, "Although the cluster described here is a community with values based on Christian beliefs, there is no reason why a cluster based on a different value system should not operate successfully. However, the support and resources of a wider community (in our case, the church) is a very significant factor which should not be underestimated." Cliff Wright appended the following observation, "The groups were of great significance to those participating, leading to many commitments personally to social action, change of jobs (less money), change of life-style, concern for children, etc." The group also provided support to its individual members who were personally involved in such organizations and activities as Action for World Development, Amnesty International, Community Aid Abroad, Australia-Korea Association, Nunwading North Neighborhood Center, Cairnmiller Emergency Foster Care Scheme, Fitzroy Center for Urban Research and Action, and the Australian Labor Party.

A second concern which emerged in both the developing and the developed countries had to do with child rearing practices. A Family Life Study Group in South Africa reported, "The focus [of our study] has been on the socialization of children in African society. The challenge facing the group is how to translate the norms and values in traditional society into modern day concepts." Two documents were discussed in the group entitled "Socialization of an African Child Through Sotho Custom" and "Socializing a Xhosa Child."

While differing in detail on the socialization process, both documents point out that the socialization of the child is the responsibility of the entire extended family and not of the parents alone. The history of the community is shared through the medium of storytelling in which the grandparents play a significant role. Uncles and aunts and other relatives also have specific responsibilities. Even the ancestors long since past are included in the various rituals of the socialization process. In ways like these the child gains a sense of security, a sense of identity, a sense of belonging, a sense of rootedness, as well as appreciation for the values and traditions of the family. The child is set within an extended community which also has a long history and memory. Puberty rites mark the transition from childhood to adulthood.

One of the reports concludes,

> Socialization builds personality and a nation; that is why stress was laid on such important ceremonies. Of course the philosophy of life is important and without having gone through these stages how can one rationalize (i.e., reason), know one's self, or even meditate or plan for the future? Gone are the good old times! How regretful!

The group's reports show considerable pain and struggle as they try to come to terms with the fact that traditional values and practices are crumbling under the onslaught of outside influences and forces as the modern world with all of its possibilities and problems imposes itself upon them.

At the other end of the spectrum of development one also finds specific concerns about the socialization of the young child particularly as this relates to the question of early childhood education where mothers are expected to be a part of the labor force. The report of the Familie '77 Wittenberg, East Germany, group included the following statement:

As generally both spouses are working, the state takes care of the education of children through a system of nurseries and kindergartens. Family education is limited to the short hours at the end of the afternoon and weekends. Parents who want to educate their children themselves are subject to an unexpressed but nevertheless very well noticed social discrimination. Mothers who interrupt their professional activities in order to educate their small children often have the feeling that they are considered by the working people to be lazy and frivolous. Production has first place in our highly industrialized state which suffers from a chronic labor shortage. Through the influence of medical doctors and pedagogues in our group, it is recommended to educate children until the age of three years in the family. This is in contradiction to the efforts of the state to reintegrate the woman into the production process soon after the birth of the child. The construction of day nurseries and kindergartens is therefore accelerated by the state.

The Finma group of Helsinki had a similar concern that the rights and duties of parents to bring up their children especially in matters concerning religion, ideology, and values be maintained.

At the moment society favors a model in which both parents are working outside the home and the children are taken care of in day care homes and kindergartens maintained primarily by the state. As society now assumes that both parents are working outside the home, the parents have less and less time for their children and children are being reared more and more in institutions. There is, therefore, the risk that political groups which happen to be in power will decide on the content of that education.

These sober looks backward from the other side of the sexual revolution should give pause for reflection to those who generally support the rights of mothers to be employed outside the home. That battle seems largely to have been won only at the expense of another right which seems now to be in jeopardy, the right of the mother not to go to work but to devote herself to the nurture of her young children.

The political settings in which the Project families found themselves ranged from chaotic to highly structured and from democratic to totalitarian regimes. The groups in Uganda lived through the terror and disruption of the closing months of Idi Amin's administration. Some literally feared for their lives if they would fill out the Project working papers in the event that they would fall into the wrong hands.

The groups in East Germany confronted the challenging task of reconciling the conflicting ideologies of Christianity and Marxism. The Wittenberg group is at home in the city of Martin Luther and heir to his religious heritage. Although the Lutheran Church is not by definition a free church, they are now having to find their way in a state which emphasizes the separation of church and state in a socialist order. Religion is seen as a private family matter which has nothing to do with public life so far as state officials are concerned.

In those countries where the political structures are highly developed such as Finland and East Germany, the groups spent considerable time reflecting on official state family policies as well as social practices affecting the family. The East German report notes that their country has the highest number of divorces in the socialist states and goes on to say, "Sexual behavior is relatively liberal even if it is against the norm of the civil and Communist ethics. Neither the church as the guardian of Christian ethics nor the Socialist Unity Party as representative of social behavior can guide this." Other areas of family policy concern have to do with housing, the care of aged parents, the problem of mentally handicapped children and adults, and the need for family counseling services.

Some of the family groups in traditional societies expressed concern that with the coming of industrialization and westernization, the strong family ties of the past were being eroded. The group in Madras, India, stated that marriage and family are held in respect and we do not have the problems of young people getting together without marriage or problems of unmarried mothers and teenage pregnancies about which we read in books and magazines from the West. There are certain traditions and values in Indian society which we have to keep up because they are good and they strengthen family life.

A strong attachment to family and kinship is something which all Indians regardless of their religious orientation have in common. Concern was expressed about Western influences which are beginning to make a strong impact on the youth, including the drug problem. There are also a number of wedding and birth traditions which many youth are rejecting including the arrangement of marriages by the parents. A number of couples in this group had arranged marriages. In their evaluation they made the following statement:

> The idea that old age has wisdom is very prevalent in India. Elderly people are given great respect according to custom and tradition; for important functions in the family, older members have to be present. Blessing from the parents and elderly members of the family are sought by younger people when they take important new steps in life. In the group we felt that Hindus still hold this as important and Christians, especially the more modern ones, tend to imitate the Western culture.... It is remarkable that when some Christian members in the group felt that Indian families also will have to face disintegration which the progressive countries are facing now when India also becomes an industrial nation, our Hindu friends felt that if we can hold on to what is good in Indian tradition that keeps families together, and if we do not lose the power within the family which has sustained the members giving them their sense of belonging and security, this disintegration need not happen to our families.

In the Philippines, the traditional marriage customs are still practiced by many including asking the hand in marriage by the spokesman of the would-be bridegroom. Premarital sexual relationships are strongly disapproved; so also is marriage between a Protestant and a Roman Catholic. The influence of the extended family is very strong in marital choice and in the marriage customs. However, the younger generation is challenging the traditional practices, and changes are taking place in such areas as who bears the financial responsibility for the wedding, interfaith marriages, and marriage in the civil courts. Some parents disinherit their children who go against their wishes in the matter of marriage and cut off all communication with them throughout their entire lifetime.

In the past, it has been traditional for as many as two to three families to live in the same house. This would include the grandparents and great-grandparents, the parental couple, and the young married couple who live in the parental home. The children are raised by all the adults in the household and come to respect the authority of older persons. This pattern, however, is beginning to change as well.

A number of groups expressed the need for developing a supporting community for their individual members and nuclear families as they seek to cope with their problems as well as to minister to others in their community. In some cases this took the form of supporting single mothers who faced economic and emotional problems. In the case of the Peace, Love and Justice group in Metro-Manila, the family cluster gathered round those persons who had family members in jail as political prisoners. They carefully monitored the results of the various court hearings that were held. Many groups provided personal support for their members who were involved in various social action projects or ministries to minority ethnic groups in their communities.

The Edinburgh East Family Group of the Iona Community has moved the farthest in the direction of a common life for its member families. These nuclear families "share a devotional and economic rule" with the larger Iona Community and fulfill their Community commitment in "devotional and economic discipline, in peacemaking, local mission, healing, and political responsibility."

The May Be Community of Darwin, Australia, reported that "we have a dream of a corporate lifestyle which has for its rules something like Micah 6:8, 'The Lord has told us what is good. What he requires is this: to do what is just, to show constant love, and to live in humble fellowship with our God.' " This is a group of three families who are deeply involved with Australian aboriginal people in the Northern Territory of Australia. They report that

> deep friendships have developed as we have shared growing concerns on such matters as justice and caring, aid to third world countries, self-determination for all peoples, community and human development, non-exploitive lifestyles (involving care of the environment which raises such questions as uranium mining, aboriginal land rights, organic gardening, etc). All have read widely and have a growing concern to live in such a way, not to opt out but to be a sign of hope that there is a way to live that shows and offers hope of a lifestyle which is not exploiting but is caring for all other people and for the Village Earth.... We are currently sending out a statement of our vision (A New Mood) to friends and acquaintances who may have some of the same frustrations and some wisdom to share with us as we continue in our search for a meaningful lifestyle and the emergence of a community of care and hope which fits in with that interpreted in Micah 6:8. ... We believe we must be open to the Spirit of God blowing where it listeth, prepared to meet any direction it seems right to go.

The "New Mood" of which they speak begins with a recital of their sense of frustration and futility but then explodes in the following affirmation:

> AND YET WE LIVE IN HOPE AND EXPECTATION BECAUSE WE SHARE A VISION OF A NEW FUTURE
> —a future in which we have the freedom to express our views openly in words and actions;
> —a future in which our ideas and convictions are integrated with our lifestyle;
> —a future in which we find new human relationships of depth

through genuine collegiality, mutual respect, the honoring of differences, the recognition of uniqueness, the full acceptance that both male and female are created in the image of God, and the valuing of children as full members of the community;
—a future in which we discover a new relationship with the earth;
—a future in which education is integrated with the whole of life, deals with the whole person and helps people to live rather than to prepare them as fodder for either the bureaucratic or the technocratic machines;
—a future in which the nuclear family is honoured but in which people reach across to others and also enter into community with those outside their families;
—a future in which some of the strengths of the religious orders are appropriated by others;
—a future in which people live in the kingdom of God rather than just talk about it;
—a future in which people "do what is just, show constant love, and live in humble fellowship with God" (Micah 6:8).

These examples, while they do not point to wide-ranging redirection of social, political, and economic forces, are examples of lighting candles in a dark world. Even a small candle can displace a lot of darkness. They are a symbol of hope that families can indeed take hold of their destiny and determine their values, their goals, and even the shape of their life together in the face of overwhelming odds. However, changing the society surrounding the family is a task of even greater proportions. The report of the Drafting Committee at the Oaxtepec meeting states:

It was discovered that effecting social change is a long slow process which requires careful strategizing and mobilizing for action, much perseverance and patience in the face of frustration and disappointment. The Project brought groups to the threshhold of action for social change by raising awareness, developing motivation, teaching a method, utilizing trial and error, and helping persons band together in a mutual reinforcement of purpose and effort.

Several things are indispensable in order to achieve effective results. There must be a clustering of families who band together with a common purpose. Many groups reported that this clustering itself gave a new sense of strength and purpose to their nuclear family life. It provided them with encouragement and support to work through the ordinary problems of family living. This mutual support is a necessary condition for initiating social change beyond the family. The goal must be clear and realistic; it must be shared by all the members of the group. There must be provision for periodic evaluation and mid-course correction.

The action/reflection model is basic to the process. Telling family stories is one of the most significant methodologies, particularly in the early phases of building the cluster. It has the effect both of building a common tradition and of helping the group assess its situation and to focus its priorities. The focus of concern must be both backward into history and forward into the future, both on its inner life and on its life in the world. It is by living in the tensions created by these polar realities that the power which families have to effect change is released.

Conclusion

We began this chapter by noting the scope and rapidity of social changes affecting family living. Some are the result of an increasing industrialization of our society; some are the product of the determined work of social engineers of various kinds. We reviewed a number of theories of what causes social change and surveyed briefly the effects on families.

The basic issue we addressed was whether families are active or passive in that process. Are they the victims of forces beyond their control? Or are they "initiating centers" for needed change? The dominant view among social scientists is that families are "dependent variables" or passive subjects. The Malta planners of the FPSC Project took the other position, that families can be the "independent variable," that they can influence social change. We can take heart from their experience.

Several years ago I entered into correspondence with a number of colleagues across the country whom I knew to be careful observers of family trends in their congregations and communities. I asked them to list these trends as they have experienced and/or observed them, to express their judgment about what further changes we may expect by the year 2000, and to identify which of these changes they were ready to affirm as hopeful signs and which caused them deep concern.

On the whole, my correspondents were fairly pessimistic about the growing individualism, secularization, and fragmentation of the family. I picked up such phrases as: "There are fewer role models of Christian family values." "We have been influenced strongly by the secular and the views of the community and world have a stronger bearing many times on decisions than church or background." "Our nonconformity has turned into conformity in our family lifestyles; our simplicity to keeping up with the Joneses." "In some . . . families, the shell of faith is present but the substance is gone. The religious values of the grandparents have been replaced by reliance on secular values and goals." "Urbanization has eroded the social milieu in which the . . . family lived so that families wishing to uphold certain traditions and values do not have the support of a [church] community as was true 25 years ago." "There is more blending in with the American values and way of life."

Others noted with optimism an increasingly critical evaluation of society's values and practices, a growing appreciation of the past, higher expectations for the quality of marriage and family relationships, greater availability of professional resources in the church and the community for marriage preparation, enrichment, and counseling along with a greater openness to seek outside help.

A number of respondents indicated that they expect to find a reexamination of family trends and a return to basic Christian values in family living. Included in this reexamination and return will be efforts to recreate the extended family in new forms ranging from koinonia groups covenanting mutual support to intentional communities. A number of persons predicted that there will be a return to simpler lifestyles partly on the basis of renewed Christian conviction about the sin of materialism and partly on the basis of the coming economic crunch and the shrinking of energy and other natural resources. Some see the greater freedom in male/female roles as a good thing and predict that the experimentation of the present time with its attending stresses and strains will have pretty well stabilized in a few years.

The bad news is that some families will continue to abandon Christian values and increasingly take on the values of the wider society. Along with this will come a sharp polarization between families. There will be families reflecting Christian commitments and those reflecting the values of secular society. There will be families who have adopted open, changing, flexible approaches and families who will revert to clearly fixed roles with clear authority patterns. It will be increasingly difficult for such families to tolerate each other in the same church.

I was cheered by a Mennonite pastor from Ontario who said, "I feel a deep optimism as I think about the future of our families. I think the next generation will be a time in which family life concentrates in an unprecedented way on relationships and personal growth and commitment to the family of humankind. In this process, God's Spirit will be moving, shaping, and leading in unpredictable ways." With the Spirit of God convicting us, nudging us, directing and guiding us, we shall yet prevail over the alien forces that would squeeze our families into their mold and a society which emphasizes individualistic self-realization even at the expense of commitment to others.

The basic task first of all is not restructuring the family but building a firm foundation of values and commitments underneath it. These values and commitments must represent those of a culture counter to the culture around us. Thus the family must be one of the churches' primary concerns; no strategy for recovering and strengthening the family apart from reference to life together in the larger family of faith will have any chance of success. To the extent that the total Christian community can stand together in maintaining its foundational values, to that extent a family life strategy can be effective. I do not have too much difficulty in rearranging the furniture of our family structures and patterns so long as the foundations are solid and sure.

5
In You All the Families of the Earth Will Be Blessed: The Mission of the Family

Now the Lord said to Abram,
"Go from your country and your kindred
and your father's house
to the land that I will show you.
And I will make of you a great nation,
and I will bless you,
and make your name great,
so that you will be a blessing.
I will bless those who bless you,
and him who curses you I will curse;
and by you all the families of the earth
shall bless themselves."
Genesis 12:1-3.

At first glance these words would seem to be a further elaboration of the theme, The Family in Transition. This was not the first time that Abram and Sarai had packed their belongings and moved their household. Nor would it be the last. Once before they had moved along with Abram's father, Terah, from Ur to Haran. Now in response to God's command, they went on the move again. This time their destination was uncertain. A second more careful look at the story of Abram and Sarai tells us that although this nomadic family is indeed entering into a long and uncertain period of transition, in a larger sense their odyssey marks a sharp reversal of direction. It is the beginning of a return, just as the expulsion of Adam and Eve from the garden was the beginning of a journey away from God. The covenant which God made with Abram and Sarai marks the beginning of God's purpose to gather a people to be his own special treasure.

In the previous chapter, we made a shift in the angle of vision with which we view the family. The family may be viewed as passive victim of outside forces working their will upon it, bending and shaping it into their various molds. We have examined a number of these influences and their impact on the family. Conversely the family may be viewed as active subject, as initiating center moving and acting upon its environment as it directs and gives shape to its chosen destiny.

The story of Abram and Sarai and their family may be read and interpreted from either of these angles of vision. One could interpret the experiences of this family on the move from the perspective of the many and various threats on its existence as they make their precarious way through foreign territory. Within a few generations they have become slaves in Egypt, totally in bondage to their Egyptian oppressors. Indeed their story has become the paradigm for contemporary analyses of social groupings who perceive themselves to be oppressed, in bondage and in need of liberation.

On the other hand, we may interpret the story of this family from the perspective of their mission to the world. This was not an ordinary tribal group in search of water and grazing land for their flocks and herds. It was a family who had entered into covenant with God and who had received a commission from him to be a blessing to the nations. Reading the story from this point of view, we see in it the fulfillment of God's purpose which does not waver and shrink in spite of all the vicissitudes of life.

The command of God and Abram's response of obedience are often quoted as the supreme example of what authentic faith looks like. See Romans 4:3, 9, 22-23; Galatians 3:6; James 2:23. What was it that Abram believed? What is the promise of the covenant that God made with him? It is that he and Sarai would have a son and through him an extended family. "Look toward heaven, and number the stars, if you are able to number them. So shall your descendants be" (Genesis 15:5). It is this promise and the seeming impossibility that it will ever be fulfilled as Abram and Sarai advance in years that provide the excitement and anticipation of this part of the book of Genesis. Nevertheless, in spite of the seeming impossibility and the severe testing of Abram's faith in God's promise, the time did come when the promise was fulfilled and Isaac was born. The faith of Abraham and Sarah (as they were renamed by God in Genesis 17) is celebrated in that great chapter of faithful men and women of God, Hebrews 11.

There is a debate in the New Testament about who are the true descendants of Abraham. Jesus, John the Baptist, and Paul took the position that God's blessing upon Abraham and his descendants extended to all who share Abraham's faith, not only his genes,(Matthew

3:9; John 8:39; Romans 4:13, 16-17). It was not intended to be narrowly restricted to those who were his literal biological descendants. There were those who took pride in their religious tradition but were too selfish to share their inheritance. But God's blessing bestowed so freely on Abraham and his descendants was not only a gift but a call to a mission. Through Abraham and his family, God was reaching out to touch all the families of the earth to bestow his blessings. The imagery of count-less stars in the heavens and innumerable grains of sand on the seashore referred not only to the number of descendants which could not be counted but to the lavish generosity of God's grace which would spill over on all families in all nations of the world.

This is the perspective with which we view the family as we conclude this study. Christians in families have a mission in the world through their families. In this chapter we shall consider several ways in which this mission may be carried out. These include (a) living for the world; (b) building a covenant marriage; (c) extend-ing the boundaries; (d) promoting authentic sexual freedom; (e) training for relationship; and (f) being a community. In its various expressions of life and work, both internal among family members and in relation to all whom they encounter in the community and the larger society, the family of Christians may carry out its mission in the world.

When we speak of a mission in the world through families, we refer not only to their words of Christian testimony and the actions of love and caring arising out of their love for Christ and the need of the neighbor. We have reference first of all to the family simply being what God intends it to be, to the family living out and fulfilling among its members and among its neighbors its essential nature as God created it. This has to do, to be sure, with *speaking* and *doing* as we shall see; even more fundamentally, however, it has to do with *being* what it is by God's design and what it may become by God's grace, that is, a covenant community of love, affection, belonging, caring, faithfulness, forgiveness, nurturance, and healing.

These good gifts are offered freely both to those who belong within its inner circles and to those whose lives it touches. At times, the pattern of its life and the actions in which it engages call for further interpretation. The covenant implicit in its life and conduct and the Christ who participates in that covenant must from time to time be interpreted explicitly. It is essential that the implicit or lived realities and the explicit interpretations be congruent with each other if the words are to be credible and the actions are to be perceived as authentic. Presence, action, and interpretation—life, deed, and word—are all essential elements in the mission of the family in and to the world.

The purposes of God's salvation have to do with overcoming alienation, with reconciliation, with relationships, with creating community. That purpose is already revealed and expressed in the relationships of the community of the family which he has given to us to nurture our personhood and teach us the lessons of belonging long before we can even lisp his name.

Living for the World

The temptation to turn inward upon themselves is a danger to modern families as well as to the descendants of Abraham. This may take the form of an overemphasis on the independence and autonomy of the nuclear family. It may take the form of preoccupation with getting and buying and spending, a consumer mentality. It may take the form of the ideology that "the greatest happiness in life is to be found in the family," one of the marks of the modern companionship family as described by Burgess and Locke. It may take the form of escapism, of giving priority to recreation, travel, and pleasure over concern for and involvement in the issues and problems of the immediate community. It may even take the form of a withdrawal from society in a futile attempt to protect the family from harmful social influences.

The Christian family has a mission to the world and must avoid the temptation to turn inward upon itself. It must have a commitment outside and beyond itself, greater even than its concern for its own survival. A family whose basic goals and lifestyle are focused inward for its own enjoyment or preservation is like a pond. A pond may become stagnant and even dry up if there are no fresh sources of water flowing into it nor any outlets for water to flow through it. A family in mission, one that lives for the world, is like a river or a stream. Fresh water from its source flows through it to carry refreshment and new life downstream as it flows onward and outward to the sea.

One way in which the Christian family can live for the world is simply to exist in the world as an example of covenant. The world needs models of covenant family living. Covenant family living has to do with the way husbands and wives look out for each other rather than seeking power or advantage for themselves. It is expressed in the way mothers and fathers give themselves to their children, loving and nurturing them and helping them develop as socially responsive and responsible persons in the neighborhood. Discouraged families can draw inspiration and take heart if they come into contact with families who build their homes on secure, permanent foundations where love and faithfulness are lived out in concrete, everyday ways. Such families can be a deep well of refreshment and strength not only for their own members but for the neighboring families as well. There are many authentic ways of showing love and care whether it is simply a cheerful "good morning," shoveling a sidewalk, and offering a ride, or whether it involves standing by or giving assistance during an illness or a crisis. We have a temptation to think of our mission in large and dramatic terms and in faraway places. As a result, we often miss the profound significance of the cup of cold water given in the name of Christ.

A second aspect of the family's mission in living for the world involves its active participation and interest in the life of its community. It is important to be informed on the issues and problems of the local community and to become involved in discussions about them and/or action in response to them. Every community has its distinctive problems, its own network of communication, and its own channels of action. A family that is totally unaware of and/or uninvolved in its community is not being faithful to its mission. A Christian witness is not authentic on the part of those who say they care but don't demonstrate that caring in shoe leather, that is, in ways that others can recognize without many words of explanation.

Active participation and involvement in local affairs has its global dimensions as well. Christian families today have the unusual privilege of being informed not only about their own community but about most or all the communities of the world. The mass media, particularly television and satellite communications systems, have made it possible for all of us to be instantly informed of significant events no matter where in the world they take place. World issues have a way of becoming local issues as well whether they have to do with the environment, energy, or population trends. On some of these issues which affect everyone in the world there are some specific actions that Christian families can take. However small and insignificant it may seem, keeping the thermostat turned down, driving under posted speed limits, or walking instead of driving have a ripple effect which can become a tidal wave.

Some issues of this nature are very complex and offer no handles for families to grasp easily. However, simply informing themselves on such issues as the inequitable distribution of wealth and consumption of the world's resources is a necessary first step in any process of change. Direct firsthand encounter with persons from the have-not countries is increasingly a possibility in our mobile world and adds the affective to the cognitive dimensions of knowing. In simpler terms, it is difficult to remain indifferent to the issues of poverty and wealth when you are confronted by the anger and despair of a poor person who holds you personally responsible for his poverty. It is difficult for most Western Christians to understand today's rhetoric of oppression, liberation, and revolution. Those persons who have looked into the eyes of a child dying from malnutrition begin to gain a glimmer of understanding and can never be the same upon their return home from a period of study, travel, or service abroad or even in the cities of North America.

An active concern for peace in the world is yet another dimension of living for the world. Again in this area the robe of peace is a seamless garment which spreads itself over the individual family, over the families in the immediate neighborhood, and all the way out to cover the families and the nations of the world. Peacemaking is a skill which is learned right at home and can be developed and practiced in both interpersonal and large corporate settings. Reading peace literature and becoming informed about strategies of peacemaking are necessary first steps to becoming peacemakers whom Jesus blessed for, he said, "they shall be called the children of God" (Matthew 5:9, KJV).

The shadow side of peacemaking is participation in picking up the pieces that are created by the devastation of war. War leaves suffering in its wake. The suffering continues long after the war makers lay down their weapons and congratulate themselves on having made peace. A vivid example of this is the desperate plight of the Vietnamese boat people who have been forced to flee their homeland. A number of local congregations are involved in helping them to make new homes in their communities. This process is a long-term one which involves not only or even primarily giving money but committing time, counsel, and friendship as these families face a totally new environment, learn a new language, and adapt to a new culture. In this vivid example we see how global and local issues merge into one and how families can become involved in world mission without even moving from their own homes.

All of the above examples are illustrations of how families can participate in the mission of the church in the world. In these and in countless other ways, the Christian family through the ministries of presence, word, and deed can share the good news of God's love in Jesus Christ. They can, of course, also participate in the formal mission program of the church through becoming informed about that program and supporting it financially and with their prayers. But that alone does not fulfill their mission. The mission strategy that God initiated in his covenant with Abraham included not only sending out his first foreign missionary family but also creating countless numbers of families in every nation of the world who would by their very presence be living testimonies of his grace and his gift.

Building a Covenant Marriage

The mission of Christians in families has both its outer and its inner dimensions. Simply to be colonies of heaven in an alien world is an essential part of their mission. For this reason, they must give careful attention to the shape and quality of their life together. As foreign embassies, they reflect the culture they have been sent to represent and interpret. Providing alternative models of marriage attractive to the people among whom they live is central to their mission.

Some persons, we noted in the second chapter, have attempted so-called radical experiments in marital patterns which have come to be characterized as "alternative intimate lifestyles." Upon closer examination, we have discovered that few of these experiments are deserving of the description "radical," since few go to the root of the matter. They are, instead, tentative attempts to experience intimacy with little commitment to partnership and permanence, to embrace tenderly while dressed in protective suits of armor. Fearing the vulnerability of commitment, they enter into "nonbinding" commitments from which they may hastily retreat should it appear to be in their interest. But authentic personal meeting, while it may be experienced in an I-Thou encounter of deeply shared intimacy, is something that goes beyond the fleeting moment and builds an enduring fabric of relationship around it. It is this fabric of relationship that we speak of as covenant.

Marriage and the family built on the basis of covenant are a truly radical alternative intimate lifestyle. It is a truly radical alternative to build a permanent relationship in a society where most things are not permanent. It is a truly radical alternative to build a marriage on faithfulness in a society where feelings, not promises, are the guiding norm for behavior. It is a truly radical alternative to place the well-being of a covenant partner at a level as high as your own in a society that stresses self-realization. It is a truly radical alternative to live in terms of self-denial rather than self-fulfillment, in giving and serving rather than in demanding and taking in a society which stresses individualism.

It is the mission of the Christian family to build marriages based on lifelong fidelity patterned after the covenant faithfulness of God with his people. It is the mission of the Christian family to model a life of giving and serving rather than demanding and taking to counteract the spirit of our age in which each one looks out for his own interests. It is the mission of the Christian family to demonstrate forgiveness and reconciliation to overcome the hatred and alienation which are tearing individuals and families and nations apart.

The covenant pattern of marriage and the family does not first of all seek its own good but the other's good. It does not demand equality but humbles itself and willingly subjects itself in love to the loved one. It does not insist on its prerogatives but freely lives in subordination. It does not assert its freedom but voluntarily gives itself in loving service. It is not individualistic but commits itself to the covenant partner.

This is how I understand Paul's analogy in Ephesians 5:21-33 of marriage as covenant. Granted, Paul is addressing himself to a culture in which men dominated the scene and controlled their wives. However, far from confirming this basically pagan pattern, I believe that Paul here presents us with a model that radically shatters the old way and sets up a Christlike pattern for leadership.

To be greatest in the kingdom, for example, is to be servant of all. The chief quality of Jesus' life and ministry is his submission; "he humbled himself and became obedient unto death, even death on a cross" (Philippians 2:8). This is the pattern for the disciple, male and female: radical submission. This is so contrary to the ways of the world that we can find no guidance from its patterns for the way a husband and wife should live together. The head of a household is not a miniature version of the head of a government or a major corporation. The biblical concept of headship has a totally different connotation for it speaks of nurture, not of power and control. It is a headship which nourishes and cherishes, which gives up itself for the sake of the beloved even to the point of dying for her. It is a headship which builds her up and has high regard and deep concern for her well-being, putting that well-being on at least as high a level of priority as its own and possibly higher. It is not a matter of superior/inferior, but of full mutuality, each outdoing the other not in privilege and prerogative but in loving service.

Not only does Paul's model challenge the patterns of the world of the first century; it also confronts and challenges the assumptions underlying the secular models of our time. It is precisely because we have followed the patterns of the world, yesterday's patterns of male domination and today's patterns of female liberation, that our families are in trouble. Paul offers a revolutionary alternative for Christian families of every age. Let us beware of rejecting what we do not even begin to understand!

The pattern that is offered here if taken seriously and applied to family relationships would go a long way toward resolving the problems our families are now facing. The question of who is boss would never arise. The distinctions of superior/inferior would never be made. Decisions would not be made on the basis of asserting self-interest but on the basis of self-giving love. Rights would not have to be demanded but would be freely offered. It is a judgment on both Christian men and women that a militant liberation spirit has arisen because of the church's failure to challenge its own cultural patterns with a radical covenant style of living.

Extending the Boundaries

A third aspect of the mission of the family is developing patterns of openness, reaching out to welcome and include others. One criticism of the church's emphasis on the family has been that single persons are excluded. Yet they, too, have been created in the image of God as sexual persons who have need for loving and caring relationships. Here we do well to recall what Paul King Jewett has said, "While marriage is perhaps the most *intimate* form of human fellowship, it is not the most *basic*. Men and women may *become* related as husband and wife, and many do; but they *are* related as men and women by virtue of God's creative act."[1] It is as women and men live in fellowship with each other that they give expression to the divine image in which they are created. They deny or distort that image when they draw back from responsible loving relationships with each other as happens, for example, when single persons are excluded from their fellowship.

Nor should we shrink from acknowledging that such fellowship is not only spiritual but also sexual in character in the most pervasive sense of that term as Rosemary Haughton has defined it. She starts out her little book *The Mystery of Sexuality* by making a distinction between *sex* and *sexuality*.

> Sex is a definite human activity, and there are many varieties of it, and many motives for engaging in it, and a vast literature connected with it—its techniques, its pleasures and the fantasies associated with it in various cultures and periods—but it is not a mystery.[2]

It is clear that Haughton is speaking of genital sex, of sexual intercourse of various kinds; as we all know and as she goes on to discuss, there is *sex* and then there is *sex*. There is good sex and there is bad sex. There is tender loving sex and there is harsh violent sex. There is committed sex and there is sex for hire and one-night stand sex. There is promiscuous sex and there is forced sex. It is important that we understand the difference and that as Christians we speak out for tender loving sex between a man and a woman who have committed their lives and their bodies to each other within a covenant of love and faithfulness in the presence of the Christian community. It is imperative that we speak out against promiscuous, exploitive, violent, and commercialized sex which makes sex objects out of persons created in God's image. However, it is equally important that we understand the difference between even good sex and sexuality, a distinction which Haughton makes clear in this definition:

> Our sexuality is not frightening or uncontrollable; it is not an idol or a slave. It is a mystery at the heart of our familiar selves; it is ourselves as we live with other people we love—parents, friends, children, lovers, husbands, wives—in individual relationships and in groups and communities.[3]

Our maleness and femaleness, our sexuality, is what reminds us that in order to exist at all we must exist in relationship, in communion and community, in fellowship, in love, in complementation, in mutuality, in belonging. This is what it means to be created in the image of God for this is how God exists and this is why he created us, for fellowship with himself and with each other. It is in this sense that sexuality goes beyond sex although the larger circle contains the smaller. Though not all persons engage in coital activity, all are sexual in this larger sense. Some choose eventually to become sexually active (i.e., through genital sexual intercourse) either in terms of what we have described as good sex or bad sex and some do not, but all are sexual beings in the sense we have described as sexuality.

Persons relate to each other not as neuters or as disembodied spirits but as females and males, as women and men. Their femaleness and maleness is not to be denied or ignored in that meeting but is an important medium of relationship. A person's femaleness or maleness is enhanced and confirmed as new levels of commonality and complementation are discovered. While all this has to do with sexuality, it does not have to do first of all with genital sexual relationship which is a particular expression of one's sexual personhood. That is fulfilled and expressed in a particular, highly focused experience of male-female relationship with one other person.

There is a complementary relationship (not a contradictory one) between the particular and the general which is similar to the relationship between sex and sexuality. The particular is only possible as an expression of the general; however, it also contributes to a person's capacity for relationships on a broader level. More specifically, if all male-female relationships were of an erotic, genital character, the result would be personal and social chaos. Community would be impossible for it would be destroyed in the maelstrom of competing, conflicting sexual impulses. It is the disciplined management of sexual drives within the setting of the biological family that makes personality and society possible. One sociologist holds that the major contribution of the family to society is the development of the incest taboo which proscribes sexual intercourse between persons who are members of the same family.

Marriage is the most intimate expression of human relationships but it stands within the larger context of relationships, the family and the community, as the smaller circle stands within the larger circle(s). The inner circle represents the most deeply intimate possibility; each concentric circle is an extension and enlargement of this intimately personal relationship. As it expands to include more persons, the depth of intimacy is somewhat diminished according to the extent of our human capacity for intimacy and the extent of the appropriate claims of others within that particular circle. Thus the inner circle is not a denial of intimacy to others further out from the center but the source upon which our capacity for intimacy with others draws.

The unmarried person draws on the intimacy of the inner circle first of all through being a child of his/her parents, one of whose basic tasks is to create a healthy emotional climate within which the growing person develops. The intimacy of the parents is not a negative factor in growing up but a deep well from which the person may draw nourishment. In like manner, the intimacy of married persons and children among whom single adults live, even though exclusive in certain respects, should not be seen as a negative factor in the relationship of singles to marrieds but as a rich and deep resource for their own lives and something to which they in turn may contribute in their way. Their relationships should become an added resource to strengthen the marriage and the families of others rather than a source of threat.

The exclusive character of sexual intimacy between the husband and wife in relation to single adults who are related to but stand outside their intimate inner circle is rooted in the Christ-church analogy. That analogy speaks about an exclusive covenant and permanent fidelity of the partners which cannot be shared outside that covenant. Beyond that, there are undoubtedly other intimacies (emotional, spiritual, physical) which may appropriately be shared beyond the marriage partners with others, particularly in the context of the fellowship of the gospel. At the same time, there will be appropriate limits to that sharing which will obviously vary from case to case. One criterion is that those things which do not violate or jeopardize the marriage covenant may appropriately be shared with others, single or married. Some persons will find much greater latitude in this principle than others.

The objection may be made that this criterion about appropriateness does not do adequate justice to the intimacy needs of those who stand outside the intimacy of marriage. This is undoubtedly true. It is also true that many married persons do not have their intimacy needs (including sexual needs) adequately met and that the differing needs and capacities of the marriage partners for sharing intimacy are often a problem. When it comes to the matter of intimacy, we must simply acknowledge that we do not live in the best of all possible worlds and that very few persons, if any (married or unmarried), have all their needs adequately met.

Nonetheless there are models of inclusion which move in the direction of a fuller celebration of the joy that is to be found in intimacy between persons, married and unmarried. Many married persons have discovered that they place an intolerable and impossible burden on each other when they demand that all their emotional needs be met by their marriage partner. Nuclear families have been weighed and found wanting in terms of their emotional resources if they are not part of a larger network of relationships. Family clusters have been developed in many countries around the world to fill a void created by the fragmentation of the extended family into smaller units in scattered places. In a few places, these have even taken the form of residential units either in adjacent housing or in common housing. Before we hastily romanticize such experiments, we would do well to recognize the enormous investment of emotional and physical energy that is required for working out the network of relationships and responsibilities in such extended households. In some places, the memory of the conflicts among members of extended families related by ties of blood is still too vivid for persons to consider these new networks. However, such realism should not be an impediment to this kind of experimentation but an incentive for hard planning and careful implementation to ensure its success.

Whether such family clusters are residential or not, an important question which arises has to do with the nature and extent of physical and emotional familiarity among the family members. The best model is the model we already have in the extended biological family in which there may be considerable emotional and physical freedom but where appropriate limits of affectionate behavior among brothers and sisters, parents and chidren, and other relatives are for the most part implicitly understood. This is part of the culture of every family though it obviously differs from one family to another. Even the meaning and forms of kissing vary from family to family as well as from culture to culture. If the family cluster is to function most freely as an emotional unit, it would do well to constitute itself in the most inclusive way, which is to say, it will consist of women and men, married and unmarried, old and young. This is the most natural form of family and best lends itself to natural physical and emotional patterns of expression.

In my view, the intimacy needs of single persons will be best met in such a familiar setting. This is especially the case if the marital relationship of the couple members of the cluster or household are strong and secure and this security is correlated with a relational context in which the traditional relational boundaries are respected. Within such a setting, there would appropriately develop considerable freedom for the expression of physical and emotional intimacy between and among all the members of the household irrespective of age, sex, or marital status.

Wherever there are intensive male-female relationships, appropriate ground rules, conventions, and symbols are created which being respected by all parties define and facilitate those relationships. Examples of these in the professional world are the white walls and white coat of the clinic, professional title and distance, the presence of secretaries and nurses, appointments which limit and focus availability, professional fees, and the like. The monogamous family system is yet another convention which sets limits and defines the nature of the relationships between persons of both sexes.

The cluster family households have yet to develop their conventions but can draw, as I have suggested, on the patterns of the biological extended family. No doubt there will be mistakes and failures in such experiments in intimacy, but then there have been and are such failures in both the professional and family settings we have described. That is not sufficient reason for abandoning the effort.

The following suggestions may be helpful to family clusters in developing guidelines for life together in the "familiar community":

(a) that the "familiar community" assume responsibility to monitor expressions of physical and emotional intimacy and to check them if there is evidence of inappropriate familiarity;

(b) that such expressions be acceptable to both single persons and married persons and their spouses and that any sense of insecurity on anyone's part be immediately respected rather than depreciated or ignored;

(c) that where there is the greatest potential for erotic attraction or deep and exclusive emotional engagement, there should be the greatest reticence, i.e., between a male and female of similar age and interest levels;

(d) that the expressions of physical affection be diffused across the larger "familiar community" and that special couple relationships (other than marriage) over an extended period of time be avoided;

(e) that physical intimacy and emotional investments be extended as generously to the "old and ugly" as to the "young and beautiful."

Promoting Authentic Sexual Freedom

A fourth aspect of the family's mission is living out, cultivating, and promoting wholesome, nonexploitive sexual patterns and relationships. Christians in families are being bombarded from all sides with alien sexual values and practices.

In describing the impact of secularism on changing sexual values, J. Richard Udry has said, "In a secular society, churches tend to reflect rather than to direct social changes."[4] Certainly the documentation that the church's influence on the sexual values and practices of our time has been significantly eroding is overwhelming. There is also considerable evidence that even church families have been drinking deeply at the fountains of a hedonistic society.

In 1928, Wilhelm Reich founded the Socialist Society for Sexual Advice and Study in Vienna, which advocated the genital sexual rights of children and young people. In the preface to the fourth edition of his book, *The Sexual Revolution,* he states that

> the forward march of the mental hygiene movement and the affirmation of the natural biological sexuality of children and young people are no longer in doubt. This movement can no longer be held back. I do not say that victory has already been won. There will still be very great clashes for decades to come. But I assert that the basic affirmation of natural love life is pressing forward and cannot be stopped despite the numerous and dangerous enemies of the living.[5]

Freedom and liberation are not the exclusive property of those who purport to speak for it in the name of the sexual revolution. These are central themes in the Christian message as well and are certainly of deep concern to Christian families as they pursue their mission in the world. Paul's letter to the Galatian Christians had freedom as its major theme—"For freedom Christ has set us free" (Galatians 5:1)—and warned of the threats to that freedom from two sides, the threat of legalism and the threat of yielding to the passions and desires of the flesh. The freedom road runs through treacherous terrain with deep ditches on either side, each pretending to be the main thoroughfare.

The sexual freedom offered by those who advocate "alternative intimate lifestyles" is not really new. The Christian congregation in Corinth encountered that same mentality in its day. It is in Paul's first letter to them in response to some specific questions and issues they were facing that some of the most explicit teachings of the New Testament about sexual relations are found. Taking the gospel to Corinth had been a daring experiment. If it could take root in such a community and transform the lives of such people, it could flourish anywhere in the world. Corinth, strategically located so that it was served by two harbors, was an important commercial center for shipping and trade. It both enjoyed the advantages and faced the problems unique to an ocean port. It was a center of great immorality; the moral standards of Corinth were lower than in the pagan world generally. On the stage of the theater in Rome, a Corinthian was usually portrayed as being drunk. To be called a Corinthian was a term of insult. To Corinthianize meant to engage in immoral relations with a prostitute. Small wonder, then, that prominent among the many problems faced by the fledgling Christian congregation there were the problems of how to reorder their personal relationships and their sexual practices in the light of the gospel.

One of the greatest challenges, though not the only one, faced by the apostles when they took the gospel to the heathen Gentiles was to work through and spell out the way in which Christian men and women were to live together as sexual beings. For example, Paul writes these rather grim words to the Christians in Corinth,

> It is well for a man not to touch a woman. But because of the temptation to immorality, each man should have his own wife and each woman her own husband. The husband should give to his wife her conjugal rights, and likewise the wife to her husband. . . . I say this by way of concession, not of command. I wish that all were as I myself am. But each has his own special gift from God, one of one kind and one of another. 1 Corinthians 7:1-3, 6-7.

The whole of chapter 7 is full of comments like that which has caused some interpreters over the years to conclude that Paul was responsible for the negative sexual bias that characterized Christian theology for many centuries. I think they are mistaken in that they fail to take two things into account. The first is the kind of situation in which the Corinthians lived and the second is the motivation underlying Paul's counsel. The motivation is not Hellenistic dualism but Paul's sense of urgency about the imminent breaking into history of the kingdom of God which was to take priority over every earthly consideration including sex and marriage. It's not that sex and marriage and the family are evil, only that they are not of the first order of things.

Against such a background, what would be the nature of responsible Christian sexual counsel? There is a certain kind of flexibility in Paul's counsel and if closely examined it is seen to be a counsel of freedom, not of rigidity. It is conservative counsel, to be sure, conservative in the best sense of the word for it is based on an understanding of sex that knows that only when it is disciplined and subordinated to a larger commitment is it truly free to yield the deepest and fullest joy it is capable of releasing.

The irony of our times so similar in many ways to first century Corinth is that when sexual license and freedom are demanded, advocated, and practiced and Christian values and standards are thrown out the window, the battles are won but the war is lost. Sexual freedom triumphs but the victory is a hollow one for it leaves only bondage and not true freedom in its wake.[6]

The threat to freedom on the other side of the road is that of legalism. This is not such a great threat today although it has been a bondage for many people (and may still be for some) with its message of repression and denial. The human sexual drive is a God-given power to be disciplined and channeled so that we may live authentically in sexual freedom, neither preoccupied with nor controlled by it.

What is authentic sexual freedom? It is the freedom to live sexually as God intended! And God intended that our sexuality become the instrument to meeting, to communion, to belonging, to reaching out, to relating, to personal existence in fellowship and in love, regarding and touching the other as subject, not exploiting the other as object, as thing to be used for my pleasure and my enjoyment.

Heini Arnold, the son of Eberhard Arnold, founder of the Society of Brothers, a modern version of the Hutterites, has written a throughly comprehensive theology of sexuality, marriage, and the family entitled *In the Image of God: Marriage and Chastity in Christian Life*.[7] In some respects this treatise seems to be coming from another century; its point of view and even its language fall at times like strange sounds on the modern ear. It is not just another modern oar dipped into the muddy and turbulent waters of marriage today. His development of a theology of the sensuous is even more striking and compelling for that reason.

By the senuous, Arnold has in mind all that we

experience through the senses of tasting, touching, seeing, smelling, and hearing along with the physical and emotional responses these activities produce. While sensuous experience is something that persons share with the animals, he notes that God expects more of us because more has been given. Arnold affirms the world of sensuous experience as right and good, though fraught with danger and offers these two safeguards: (a) Does it glorify God? (b) Is it shared with another person? In other words, if it is experienced as idolatry or selfishness, if it separates from God or from others, it is sin.

The sensuous nature of sexual experience, in Arnold's view, is distinct from other sensuous experience in that it reaches more profoundly into the human personality. It is more vitally connected to "the deeper experiences of mind and spirit" and "penetrates to the very roots of man's physical being and directly into his soul."

> The sensual sphere in its sexual aspect has a central place in man because first of all body and soul and spirit meet here as they do in no other area of experience. The sexual life affects the spirit, heart, and soul of man in a very deep sense. Secondly, the sexual life has an intimacy all its own, which the individual instinctively hides from others.[8]

Sexual love, says Arnold, is not only a physical act but a spiritual act. Its goal is union; its desire is the full giving of the self to the other. It is an expression of love, a symbol of communion with God. It is not to be seen first of all as a means to an end—procreation—but as a uniting of two people who become one in spirit, soul, and body. There must be an inner participation corresponding to the external uniting of two bodies or it becomes sin even for married people. The task, then, is to enter into sensuous experience, including sexual love, under the blessing and permission of God and under the control of the Spirit of God who overcomes the danger of being swallowed up by the purely sexual sphere.... Only the Holy Spirit holds this sovereignty and brings God's blessing in the most sensuous moments.[9]

The determination of various liberation movements to change long established values and practices is evidence of the ability of persons of strong conviction to turn things around. Whatever one may think of their goals, Christian families can certainly learn from their efforts. They are characterized by belief in the rightness of their cause, readiness to speak up and speak out forcefully, perseverance and patience, recognizing that theirs is a long-term battle, a careful assessment of the enemies and obstacles that lie in their way, refusal to become discouraged, and confidence in the ultimate triumph of their effort. They are organized as a movement which implies both momentum and a joining of efforts to provide mutual support and encouragement and to reinforce the impact of their various initiatives. They use every possible medium to gain the attention of society in their attempts to persuade.

These strategies are certainly worthy of consideration by Christian families who have another vision of the goal of authentic sexual freedom. But even more powerful than this is the willingness of Christians to live in the sexual freedom that arises out of the covenant understanding of sexuality, marriage, and the family and to pass on that understanding quietly to their children and grandchildren who grow up in their families.

Training for Relationship

The mission of the family also includes an educational task which it cannot escape. Although it is not a school in a formal sense, it educates just by being a family, that is, a group of persons who belong together, a community. The family may fail to carry out this task effectively (just as there is good education and poor education and even miseducation) but educate it must. Emil Brunner puts the matter succinctly in these words:

> It belongs to the divine order in creation that the child should grow up in the bosom and under the protection of the family, not merely as a physical being—for that is a false abstraction—but as a person. Here the child learns (what is more important than anything else it can learn) to know in an exemplary way the fundamental relation of community, the sense of connexion through the mutual need of one another, the connexion which consists in being "over against" one another, the recognition of the other as one who is unlike myself, whom I am obliged to recognize just because he is unlike. What the child learns in this intercourse with his father and mother, is far more important than anything that he can learn in school—and this is true even if his parents are not ideal but only tolerably satisfactory. The essential thing in the family is not a material or spiritual something but the actual fact of community. In family life the person is always present as a whole and counts as a whole. The family is not a school: it is community, even if it is this only in a relative and imperfect sense. It is this which is the incomparable element in the bond which unites the individual members of the family to each other. The responsibility of the one for the other, the sense of a mutual bond and a mutual obligation, which this responsibility implies, in spite of all imperfection, is still present, in some way or another, even in an only semi-decent family, in a way which exists nowhere else.[10]

Educators have become increasingly aware of the significance of informal learning, that is, the kind of learning that goes on when no one is consciously setting out to teach anything. Motivation is a crucial factor in learning and in school education, which is built around curricula and textbooks and takes place in classrooms according to a schedule. The teacher has to build motivation to learn if it is not already present. Carl Rogers is persuaded that we could teach everything in the curriculum in one-third the time if we could learn how to present the material at the teachable moment, that is, at the point of the student's readiness to learn in terms of capacity and motivation.[11] For example, notice how quickly even slow learners master the complex skills of learning to drive a car.

Learning in the family is more like learning to drive a car than like learning arithmetic or chemistry. We saw earlier how a small child learns a complex set of skills called language long before he goes to school simply by living in the family. This happens not by sitting down with a book and a teacher but by responding in various ways to the people who talk with the child. Much encouragement and reinforcement of effort are given in response to the child's efforts but there is a built-in motivation to learn to communicate as well. Communication is a fundamental part of any relationship and the growing child thrives and grows on relationships.

The complex of interpersonal relationships we call the family not only uses language to communicate; it is itself a language. Reuel Howe calls this "the language of relationships."[12] There are, he says, two popular misconceptions about the character of language. One is that communication (and teaching) is primarily verbal; the second is that a word bears its own meaning within itself. In fact, words are in great measure subjective; we each bring our own experiences to bear upon our understanding of a word. The word "family" is a good case in point.

The meaning of a word is grounded in experience; human experience is, therefore, prerequisite to the understanding of its meaning. This can be illustrated by reference to the word "trust." Trust cannot be taught; it must be awakened in the course of living with persons who can be trusted. Only then does the verbal symbol take on any meaning for a person. The Spirit of God sanctifies human relationships and through them facilitates communication between persons and between persons and God. The language of relationships and the language of words must be correlated if meaningful communication is to take place.

The home initiates the growing child into the use of the church's language primarily at the point of the experiences in relationship out of which words grow. In addition to the word "trust," all other basic words in the Christian vocabulary such as love, faith, forgiveness, hope, reconciliation, grace, joy, peace, patience, kindness, goodness, gentleness, self-control grow out of relationships in the Christian home. They must be experienced before they can be meaningfully verbalized. These are, for the most part, words of relationship. Love and acceptance, so crucial to every human being, are needs from the moment of birth until the moment of death. These needs are first satisfied in the relationship with parents; if they are not adequately met in that relationship and in subsequent relationships in the family, the person may find it difficult to show love and acceptance to others in later years.

It is also important to the growing child that the relationship between parents be one of love and acceptance in order to grow up with a sense of security. Yet parental love and acceptance (as are all human love and acceptance) are partial, finite, and limited. Parents cannot love perfectly even though they may want to because their own need for love makes it impossible to love others selflessly. Besides, the desire to love perfectly is frequently weakened by the fact that the child may be most unlovable at the very time he most needs to be loved. Even at best, says Howe, no parents are fully able to accept their child, welcoming without reservation the new demands and claims that the newly born infant makes and the disruption in the family's routine that is created.

What is the answer to this dilemma? The answer is that God's love and acceptance in Christ break into this vicious circle of insecurity and ambivalence injecting hope into a hopeless situation. By faith as parents we can lay hold on God's gift of love ("We love, because he first loved us," 1 John 4:19) which transcends our human limitations and flows through us as the human medium of God's love for our children. If our human love were perfect, we would have no need for God. At a certain point both parent and child must recognize their limitations and look to God, who alone can love them perfectly and accept them fully. The ultimate source of love, acceptance, and forgiveness is in God. As parents we can lead our children toward God by loving them even in fragmentary ways and by acknowledging to them that God is the source of our loving. Of course, our children do not automatically become members of God's family of faith simply by growing up in a human family, not even in a Christian family. Just as we are born by physical birth into a human family, so we must be born by spiritual birth into God's family.

The Christian family cannot guarantee that this will happen. It can, however, be a place where God is experienced. The Christian family points beyond itself to a larger family, the family of faith, for it is an analogy of the household of God. But it not only points; it also prepares the growing person for the experience of those larger relationships. It becomes the training ground for true spiritual community because the lessons and the language of relationship it teaches are basic for the life of faith.

Education in the family stands in a complementary (not competitive) relationship to the educational program of the schools. The family is a small group in which the emotional bond between the members is deep and more or less permanent although it shifts its character throughout the various developmental stages. Even so, the relationships are normally lifelong and they are of a primary, rather than a secondary, character. That is to say, persons come together in that setting not first of all to educate each other or for the sake of providing certain goods and services on a contractual basis. That education happens and that goods and services are exchanged we do not deny, but the constitutive basis for the family lies in the fact that it is a community of affection; it is a place where one belongs. It is this that is the family's greatest strength and which conditions the quality of the education it provides.

I have not, I acknowledge, dealt with the problem of broken families or dependent families who seem to have so few resources in themselves simply to cope with life in a complex and fast-changing world. I am assuming a measure of stability in the situation and the presence of love by the members for one another. Where these are significantly absent we are talking not about *education* but about *therapy* or other supportive ministries by the church and community agencies. In any case, let us not overestimate the quality of relationships in any of our so-called "better" families, nor underestimate the measure of love and security which may spring forth unexpectedly in families where we do not look to find it. In the final analysis, it is the inbreak of God's healing grace in surprising ways in unlikely places which keeps all of us humble and draws forth our gratitude.

Being a Community

Finally, in the last aspect of the mission of the family we shall consider, we emphasize once again the profound significance of the family simply being what God created it to be, a community of persons in relationship. Here persons may learn the most basic lesson in life: that our lives are bound up with others, that we are made for relationship.

In our discussion of the family in transition in the previous chapter, we noted how susceptible the family is to social, economic, and political influences which profoundly shape its life. We also noted that some persons and families are convinced that that influence is not a one-way street only, that the family also has power to shape its environment. Emil Brunner sees this reciprocity or interdependence as arising out of the fact that all of us live simultaneously within the natural forms of community which arise out of and take shape within the sexual, social, economic, and political spheres of life. "We know them as means by which the divine wisdom *compels* men to live in community—men, that is, who through their sin have become separated from one another, and in their inmost will have lost the sense of corporate life."[13] In other words, each of the natural forms of community is founded on the same basic principle, that people need each other in order to exist; each is an expression in its own way of the human drive toward community.

Brunner identifies five natural forms of community: the community of labor; the community of the people and of law; the community of culture; the community of life (marriage and the family); and the community of faith. It may seem a bit surprising that he should include the church as one of the natural forms of community for surely the church as the people of God has a transcendent dimension that is not equally the case with the other communities in his list. However, "we have this treasure in earthen vessels" as Paul has said and James Gustafson has demonstrated in his sociological analysis of the church in a book by that title. Like other human communities, the church has a history, a common language, a political structure, a distinct membership, and the like. Viewed from the perspective of faith, it must, of course, be recognized that the church as the body of Christ is more than these but certainly it is not less.

At the heart of each of these natural communities, like the seed to the plant, is the living principle which brings them to life, what Brunner calls "community itself." It exists only in the immediacy of the meeting between the "I" and the "Thou." "In the strict sense of the word, there is only one form of community: union in love."[14] "Community itself" is fully personal meeting, the mutual disclosure or self-revelation of the "Thou," with no other end in view; the natural forms or expressions of community arise out of and are based upon a common interest, purpose, or idea. Of course, the personal element is never completely absent from the various human structures of community. When a common idea, purpose, or thing draws persons together, the possibility of true personal meeting, of "community itself," is always present.

> The natural forms of community are thus not merely parables, analogies of true community, but they are also the means of a divine training for community. Through them, *nolens volens*, man is placed within society, has its claims laid upon him, and is shown the meaning of true community.... Everywhere in the natural state of life in community he discovers an anticipation of that which faith tells him is the meaning of human life; that is co-existence, dependence on others, and the fact that we owe our very being to others. What the natural human reason recognizes as "virtually necessary regulations" ... faith regards as the ordering of the Divine Goodness in Creation, by means of which he gives us life, through which he gives us to each other, requires us to live for one another, and thus educates us for a life in common.[15]

The community of life (i.e., of marriage and the family) stands apart from and prior to the communities of labor, the law, and culture in two respects. It is in the family that a person first experiences community with the result that later experiences in the other communities (this would be true also of the community of faith) are greatly conditioned by the earlier ones. Also, except for the community of faith, the community of marriage and the family more than any other exists for the sake of and leads most directly to the personal relationship which constitutes "community itself." At the heart of the family is the love relationship between husband and wife; at its best, they experience from time to time that ecstasy of pure personal meeting in which each is disclosed fully to the other, what Buber calls the "I-Thou relationship." Brunner asserts that "from this experience, more than from any other, the truth gradually dawns upon us that we, as human beings, were never meant to lead a solitary existence."[16]

It is this priority of the family among the various forms of community which makes "family" an appropriate definition of community wherever it is found. Johannes Pederson, in discussing the social cohesiveness of Israel in the Old Testament period, notes that the term "family" served equally well to denote the household, tribal, or national unit.[17] Several Hebrew words—*mishpāhā, hayyā, 'eleph,* and *ām*—are used to designate the various units, each of which is wider in scope than the previous one—household, tribe, people. All can, however, be rendered "family" and the term *mishpāhā* can be used to designate any of these communities. The line of distinction between them was necessarily fluid because each was an expression of the same fundamental reality. The reality expressed was, of course, not that of biological kinship but that kinship of spirit which goes even deeper than blood relationship.

> ... (The term) family, *mishpāhā,* is the designation of those who are of the same kind, have the same essential features, and it is the essential factor of the community.... All that forms a whole, a homogeneous community with its own characteristics, is a *mishpāhā* ... the idea of the *mishpāhā* is the basis of all definitions and ... immediately presents itself whenever the Israelite wants to define a community.... So flexible is the term *mishpāhā*

that it can be used wherever there is a whole bearing the impress of a common character.... And the family not only expands in scope so as to comprise all of those who share in the common characteristics: it comprises all of the same stamp throughout the ages.[18]

Similarly, the New Testament uses family or household images to describe the belongingness or relatedness of persons who are bound together in Christ, for example, sons of God, brothers and sisters, a wedding feast, the bride of Christ, the household of God, God as Father. Even the words of Jesus in Luke 8:19-21, "My mother and my brothers are those who hear the word of God and do it," gives us an example of the elastic use of the concept of family rather than being a case of pitting the larger use of the term against the more limited one. Perhaps the most vivid illustration of the interconnectedness of the human family with the family that God is creating is the startling similarity between the relationship of Christ with his church and between a husband and wife. See Ephesians 5:21-33.

There is, then, within the family a reality which is embodied in all the natural forms of community including the church. This reality is more than the natural basis of community; its significance extends beyond these natural forms for it provides the basis for an analogy of the relation between God and his people, Christ and his church. The family always points beyond itself: in one direction it points to its solidarity with other natural communities; in the other direction, it points to the divine-human community which is both the source and the norm of community wherever it is experienced and to whatever degree.

The family then has as part of its mission in the world the vocation to embody and to point toward "community itself." Stripped of many of its other functions by its growing dependence on other structures and agencies, it continues to exist primarily for meeting one's most intimate personal needs, needs which can be satisfied only in a loving network of intimate relationships. Not that the family, any family, is or can become a perfect expression of community! Indeed, experiences of full personal meeting where we are recognized and loved solely for who we are, not what we can do, are rare, transitory, and fleeting. However, our insatiable need for intimacy keeps us within the community of the family. Brunner interprets this need for intimate relationship with others as the mark of the Creator and sees in it the foundational principle of all natural communities, including the family. As a broken imperfect community in the midst of broken imperfect communities, the family can only, as Brunner puts it, live off the divine forgiveness.

Community is both a gift and a task. Wherever it is experienced, within the family and beyond it, it is the gift of God, sheer grace. But it is also and at the same time a task. It is very important that we appreciate this dialectic of both receiving gratefully and laboring diligently, for it is in this creative tension that we experience God's gift. The task involves both the inner ordering of life together in the family and its relationship to the world around it. The task includes the family's symbolic function of pointing to a reality beyond itself; its very existence is an analogy of God's relationship to his people, of Christ with his church. Secondly, the task includes an educational function, of being the "school" of community. In this school we learn that we do not exist by, of, or for ourselves but that our life is bound up in and with each other. Finally, the family may even participate in that communion of God with persons which he desires to give us as his gift. Its earthly institutional expression is the church; it may also be experienced within the family for Jesus said that "where two or three are gathered in my name, there am I in the midst of them" (Matthew 18:20).

Conclusion

We have been discussing the mission of the Christian family in the world. The components of that mission include:

(a) *living for the world* as Christ lived for the world, avoiding the temptation to turn inward upon itself or to withdraw from its responsibility to be by its very presence a living example of God's love and grace;

(b) *building a covenant marriage* in which society's patterns both of domination and of liberation are rejected in favor of a style of life in which each one actively seeks the good of the other and is committed to faithfulness and permanence;

(c) *extending the boundaries* of love and fellowship to include others who do not stand within the immediate circle of intimacy;

(d) *promoting authentic sexual freedom* in which both sex and sexuality do not become exploitive and possessive but become the instrument to meeting, to relating, to communion, to belonging, to personal existence in fellowship and love, regarding the other not as object but as subject;

(e) *training for relationship* in which the lessons and the language of relationship so basic to the life of faith are lived and taught;

(f) *being a community* in which God's purpose for how we should live together in all human structures is first experienced and learned.

We may well ask whether the family as we know it today is capable of taking on such a mission. In any case, are these not elements of the mission of the church? Indeed they are! Nor would any family all by itself be capable of carrying out this mission if it were not surrounded by other families in the church drawing on its resources. The point is not to set the family over against the church, a false dichotomy. The point is rather to view the church and its mission from the perspective of the primary setting within which its members live out their life in the world.

A basic strategy of the church in carrying out its

mission is to think of itself as a family of families, an extended family of brothers and sisters, parents and children. We noted earlier the richness of family images in the New Testament which are used to describe the nature of the church. Since the church, like the family, faces the temptation to turn inward upon itself rather than to live for the world around it, it must deliberately take measures to avoid that danger and to engage actively in its mission. If its member families are provided the resources to fulfill their mission, the congregational family will at the same time be carrying out its mission.

There are, to be sure, several elements in the mission of the church which go beyond the mission of the family. These include the proclamation of the Word, the formal teaching of the Scriptures, and the celebration of the Lord's Supper. In ways like these, the church communicates the grace of God through its service of worship, study, and prayer to its member families who then are privileged to incarnate the life of faith in their households.

No discussion of the mission of the family in the world can be complete without taking into account the startling, even harsh words of Jesus recorded in Luke 14:26, "If anyone comes to me and does not hate his own father and mother and wife and children and brothers and sisters, yes, and even his own life, he cannot be my disciple"; and in Matthew 10:34-35 about having come "to set a man against his father, and a daughter against her mother, and a daughter-in-law against her mother-in-law"; and in Matthew 10:37 that "he who loves father or mother more than me is not worthy of me."

Are we to understand Jesus as a hatemonger, a destroyer of relationships, a sower of discord in families with the purpose of breaking them up? Such would seem to be the literal meaning of his words. How could such a message be reconciled with his larger message of healing love, forgiveness, and reconciliation in human relationships?

There is a similar puzzle in the writings of Paul in 1 Corinthians 7:29-31.

> I mean, brethren, the appointed time has grown very short; from now on, let those who have wives live as though they had none, and those who mourn as though they were not mourning, and those who rejoice as though they were not rejoicing, and those who buy as though they had no goods, and those who deal with the world as though they had no dealings with it. For the form of this world is passing away.

How is it possible for those who are married to live as though they were unmarried? Surely Paul is not condoning irresponsibility in marital relationships! How is it possible for those who buy to live as though they had no goods and those who rejoice as though they were not rejoicing? This calls for a kind of balancing act few of us have mastered. It refers to the kind of paradox or tension with which the Christian is called to live in the world. We must live in it fully with both feet firmly on the ground if we are to live responsibly and not always be dreaming about tomorrow and somewhere else. We plant our grain and build our barns and marry and raise children and laugh and cry as though we will be here forever. At the same time we remember that we have been addressed by God, called into his family by faith in Jesus Christ, that our citizenship is in heaven, and that the end time is breaking into the present even now. It is because of this tension that we cannot settle in and settle down permanently where we are. In the midst of growth and change, of buying and selling, of marrying or not marrying, of bearing and rearing children, we keep alert and hold ourselves in readiness for the call of God.

What this text has in common with the apparently

harsh words of Jesus about family relationships is the absolute necessity of maintaining the priority of the kingdom of God. The human family, like all other things in this earthly existence, must not take on in our lives the place that rightfully belongs to God alone. I do not understand this to mean that these loving relationships are evil in themselves. I do understand it to mean that for people who live in covenant, loyalty to the kingdom of God takes first place. It is another of God's mysterious gifts to his children that when they forsake all for the kingdom, what they receive back from him is greatly enriched. So when we are ready to lose our life for the kingdom, we find it truly for the first time. Those families who, taking their covenant seriously, give God first place ahead even of their family relationships and obligations discover a deeper joy and a greater stability in those very relationships than they would have otherwise known. "Seek first his [God's] kingdom and his righteousness and all these things shall be yours as well" is as true in family life as in any other area of kingdom living.

Notes

Chapter 1

1. Vance Packard, *The Sexual Wilderness* (New York: David McKay, 1968), p. 15.

2. Quoted in Mary Daly, *Beyond God the Father* (Boston: Beacon Press, 1973), p. 44. Daly's is an angry book as she herself acknowledges in the Preface. It is a total rejection of the language, images, institutions, and assumptions of traditional Judeo-Christian thought in search of a new frame of reference structured by women. "As aliens in a man's world who are now rising up to name—that is, to create—our own world, women are beginning to recognize that the value system that has been thrust upon us by the various cultural institutions of patriarchy has amounted to a kind of gang rape of minds as well as of bodies" (p. 9). Though much more amicable in her approach, Letty M. Russell, *Human Liberation in a Feminist Perspective: A Theology* (Philadelphia: Westminster Press, 1974) and *The Future of Partnership* (Philadelphia: Westminister Press, 1979), retains the language of oppressed (women) and oppressor (men). However she sees these as systemic rather than personal categories and calls upon women and men to collaborate in building the partnership of the future.

3. James B. Nelson, *Embodiment: An Approach to Sexuality and Christian Theology* (Minneapolis: Augsburg, 1978), p. 56. For fuller historical documentation of this subject, see also D. S. Bailey, *Sexual Relation in Christian Thought* (New York: Harper & Bros., 1959); Donald F. Winslow, "Sex and Anti-Sex in the Early Church Fathers" and Eleanor L. McLaughlin, "Male and Female in Christian Tradition: Was There a Reformation in the Sixteenth Century?" in Ruth Tiffany Barnhouse and Urban T. Holmes, III, eds., *Male and Female: Christian Approaches to Sexuality* (New York: Seabury Press, 1976).

4. John Money and Patricia Tucker, *Sexual Signatures: On Being a Man or a Woman* (Boston: Little, Brown, and Co., 1975), p. 14. Although Johns Hopkins was among the first U.S. institutions to pioneer in performing transsexual surgery, it stopped doing so (at least temporarily) in June, 1978, after a follow-up study of its patients conducted by Dr. Jon K. Meyer, director of its Sexual Behaviors Consultation Unit. He presented his unpublished paper to a meeting of the American Psychiatric Association in Toronto in 1977 in which he concluded that there were no significant differences in adjustment between those who had undergone surgery and those who had not.

5. *Ibid.*, p. 9.

6. *Ibid.*, p. 16.

7. *Ibid.*, p. 73.

8. *Ibid.*, p. 66.

9. John Money and Anke A. Ehrhardt, *Man and Woman, Boy and Girl: The Differentiation and Dimorphism of Gender Identity from Conception to Maturity* (Baltimore: Johns Hopkins University, 1972), p. 147.

10. Money and Tucker, p. 230.

11. Janet Saltzman Chafetz, *Masculine, Feminine, or Human? An Overview of the Sociology of the Gender Roles* (Itasca, Ill.: F. E. Peacock Publishers, Inc., 1978), p. 37.

12. The latest such study, The Framingham (Mass.) Study, conducted by the U.S. federal government stated that "women who work do not have any more heart disease, on the average, than women who stay home, despite the often-voiced fear that as women work more, they will be less healthy and lead shorter lives. Although 42 percent of the work force is now female, there is on the whole no evidence yet that women have been losing their survival advantage over men" (*International Herald Tribune*, January 28, 1980).

13. Shirley Weitz, *Sex Roles: Biological, Psychological and Social Foundations* (New York: Oxford University Press, 1977), p. 12.

14. Money and Tucker, p. 47.

15. Weitz, p. 41.

16. *Ibid.*, p. 3.

17. *Ibid.*, p. 207.

18. *Ibid.*, p. 248.

19. *Ibid.*, p. 248.

20. *Ibid.*, p. 249. The quotation is from Shulasmith Firestone, *The Dialectic of Sex* (New York: Bantam, 1971).

21. Chafetz, pp. 236-7.

22. *Ibid.*, p. 249.

23. Money and Tucker, p. 234.

24. *Ibid.*, p. 235.

25. Janet T. Spence and Robert L. Helmreich, *Masculinity and Femininity: Their Psychological Dimensions, Correlates and Antecedents* (Austin: University of Texas, 1978), p.l8.

26. *Ibid.*, p. 118.

27. Dr. Barnhouse's article is contained in an anthology which she coedited with Urban T. Holmes, III, *Male and Female: Christian Approaches to Sexuality* (New York: Seabury Press, 1976), pp. 3-13.

28. David R. Mace, *The Christian Response to the Sexual Revolution* (Nashville: Abingdon Press, 1970), pp. 71-88.

29. Paul King Jewett, *Man as Male and Female* (Grand Rapids: Eerdmans, 1975), pp. 23ff.

30. *Ibid.*, p. 23.

31. Chafetz, p. xii.

32. Jewett, p. 24.

33. Letty M. Russell, *The Future of Partnership* (Philadelphia: Westminster Press, 1979), pp. 49-50.

34. *Ibid.*, p. 50.

35. *Ibid.*, pp. 51-53.

36. Chafetz, pp. 252-3.

37. Emil Brunner, *The Word and the World* (New York: Charles Scribner's Sons, 1931), p. 114.

Chapter 2

1. Roger W. Libby and Robert N. Whitehurst, *Marriage and Alternatives: Exploring Intimate Relationships* (Glenview, Ill.: Scott, Foresman and Co., 1977), p. xxi.

2. John McMurtry, "Monogamy: A Critique," *Marriage and Alternatives*,

edited by Libby and Whitehurst, p. 3.

3. *Ibid.*, p. 7.

4. *Ibid.*, p. 7.

5. A second volume similar to Libby and Whitehurst in many respects is Bernard I. Murstein, ed., *Exploring Intimate Life Styles* (New York: Springer Publishing Co., 1978).

6. Charles Lee Cole, "Cohabitation in Social Context," *Marriage and Alternatives*, edited by Libby and Whitehurst, p. 67.

7. *Ibid.*, p. 66.

8. *Ibid.*, p. 75.

9. Christopher Lasch, *Haven in a Heartless World: The Family Besieged* (New York: Basic Books, 1977), p. 139.

10. *Ibid.*, p. 139.

11. Robert H. Rimmer, "Being in Bed Naked with You is the Most Important Thing in My Life," *Marriage and Alternatives*, edited by Libby and Whitehurst, p. 361.

12. *Ibid.*, p. 361.

13. David Mace and Vera Mace, "Counter-Epilogue," *Marriage and Alternatives*, edited by Libby and Whitehurst, p. 391.

14. John F. Cuber and Peggy B. Harroff, "Foreword," *Marriage and Alternatives*, edited by Libby and Whitehurst, p. xiv.

The book in which this essay appeared is not quite an objective, dispassionate scholarly attempt to describe what is called "the search for intimacy in a variety of life-styles over a lifetime" (p. 386) although in some sense it aspires to be that through all the scholarly studies it cites and the scholarly apparatus it employs to document its conclusions. Libby states his point of view and his ethical criterion explicitly in the Epilogue, "In the book we have assumed choice of a life-style to be the legitimate right of each human being. It is important to ask oneself: 'Does this relationship make me happy?' (as well as to consider the consequences of the relationship to others" (p. 386). The book is committed to advocacy not of a particular pattern of sexual intimacy but to making known the wide range of intimate alternatives along with some evaluation of their rewards and their costs. It is dedicated "to those who choose to explore intimacy within and beyond marriage."

The editors and the writers make it clear that they are not simply advocating a hedonistic approach to sexual expression. The alternative lifestyles movement, they say, is based on a more broadly based philosophy which it shares in common with other liberation movements. In particular, they express the indebtedness of the movement to the Humanist Statement on Sexual Rights and Responsibilities drafted by Lester A. Kirkendall and others (p. 378).

15. James B. Nelson identifies one of the most crucial tasks of a theology of sexuality as being the exploration of the problem of sexual alienation, a universal problem common to all cultures and traditions, including Western culture and the Judeo-Christian tradition. Sexual alienation has expressed itself in two dualisms: sexist dualism and spiritualistic dualism. Sexist dualism manifested itself in "the subordination of women—systematically present in the institutions, the interpersonal relations, the thought forms, and the religious life of patriarchal cultures" (*Embodiment*, p. 46). Spiritualistic dualism posed a dichotomy between

the spirit and the body. The higher life to which all were urged to aspire was the life of reason, of contemplation, of the aesthetic; the lower realm to be avoided insofar as possible was life in the body, that is, the life of the physical appetites and drives, passion, emotion, and desire. Nelson shows how these two dualisms interpenetrated and reinforced each other in the subordination of women in that historically men tended to identify themselves with the qualities of reason and spirit and to identify women with the qualities of emotion and sensuality. Because of this "natural" superiority, men "believed themselves destined to lead both civil and religious communities" (*Ibid.,* p. 46).

16. James Burtchaell, *Marriage Among Christians: A Curious Tradition* (Notre Dame, Ind.: Ave Maria Press, 1977), p. 11.

17. Robert N. Whitehurst, "The Monogamous Ideal and Sexual Realities," *Marriage and Alternatives,* edited by Libby and Whitehurst, p. 17.

18. Quoted by Robert W. Libby in "Epilogue," *Marriage and Alternatives,* edited by Libby and Whitehurst, p. 372.

19. Emil Brunner, *The Divine Imperative,* trans. Olive Wyon (London: Lutterworth Press, 1942), pp. 344-5.

20. Harry Stack Sullivan, *The Interpersonal Theory of Psychiatry* (New York: W. W. Norton, 1953),p. 34.

21. McMurtry, "Monogamy: A Critique," *Marriage and Alternatives,* edited by Libby and Whitehurst, p. 8.

22. Rustum Roy and Della Roy, "Is Monogamy Outdated?" *Marriage and Alternatives,* edited by Libby and Whitehurst, p. 25.

23. Jewett, *Man as Male and Female,* p. 132.

24. *Ibid.,* p. 131.

25. *Ibid.,* p. 112.

26. See, for example, D. S. Bailey, *The Mystery of Love and Marriage* (New York: Harper & Bros., 1952).

27. Gibson Winter, *Love and Conflict: New Patterns in Family Life* (New York: Doubleday, 1957), p. 102.

28. *Ibid.,* p. 103.

29. Bailey, *The Mystery of Love and Marriage,* p. 53.

30. Winter, p. 103.

31. Bailey, *The Mystery of Love and Marriage,* p. 44.

32. Roger W. Libby, "Epilogue," p. 384.

33. John Meyendorff, *Marriage: An Orthodox Perspective* (New York: St. Vladimir's Seminary Press, 1975), p. 17.

34. *Ibid.,* p. 19.

Chapter 3

1. Quoted by Weitz, *Sex Roles,* pp. 244-5, from A. S. Rossi, ed., *The Feminist Papers* (New York: Columbia University, 1973), p. 533.

2. Quoted by Weitz, p. 249, from C. Guettel, *Marxism and Feminism* (Toronto: Women's Press, 1974), p. 39. The original statement is apparently in Shulasmith Firestone, *The Dialectic of Sex* (New York: Bantam, 1971), which was not available to me at the time of this writing.

3. Burtchaell, *Marriage Among Christians,* p. 39.

4. *Ibid.,* p. 39.

5. Nelson, *Embodiment*, p. 71.

6. *Ibid.*, p. 55.

7. Roland H. Bainton, *What Christianity Says About Sex, Love and Marriage* (New York: Association Press, 1957), p. 16.

8. *Ibid.*, p. 18.

9. *Ibid.*, pp. 91-9.

10. Otto Piper, *The Biblical View of Sex and Marriage* (New York: Charles Scribner's Sons, 1960), p. 35.

11. *Ibid.*, pp. 41-2.

12. *Ibid.*, p. 41.

13. Quoted by Weitz, p. 228, from A. G. Leijon, *Swedish Women—Swedish Men* (Stockholm: Swedish Institute, 1968), p. 145.

14. U.S. Bureau of the Census, *Statistical Abstract of the United States: 1980* (Washington, D.C., 1980), p. 394.

15. Quoted in *New York Times*, September 2, 1981, p. 15.

16. Lasch, *Haven in a Heartless World*, p. 25.

17. *Ibid.*, p. 4.

18. *Ibid.*, pp. 3-4.

19. Money and Tucker, *Sexual Signatures*, p. 100.

20. Weitz, pp. 60ff.

21. James Gustafson, *Treasure in Earthen Vessels* (New York: Harper & Bros., 1961), p. 10.

22. Reuel Howe, *Man's Need and God's Action* (New York: Seabury Press, 1953), pp. 96, 128.

23. Paul S. Minear, "Work and Vocation in Scripture," *Work and Vocation: A Christian Discussion*, ed. John Oliver Nelson (New York: Harper & Bros., 1954), p. 46.

24. Ernest W. Burgess and Harvey J. Locke, *The Family: From Institution to Companionship*, 2nd ed. (New York: American Book Company, 1960), pp. 240-62.

Chapter 4

1. Bernard I. Murstein, *Love, Sex and Marriage Through the Ages* (New York: Springer Publishing Co., 1974), p. 14.

2. *Ibid.*, p. 12.

3. *Ibid.*, p. 10.

4. Lasch, *Haven in a Heartless World*, p. 26.

5. Burgess and Locke, *The Family: From Institution to Companionship*, p. 22.

6. Talcott Parsons, "The Social Structure of the Family," *The Family: Its Function and Destiny*, ed. Ruth Nanda Anshen (New York: Harper & Bros., 1959), p. 242.

7. *Ibid.*, p. 250.

8. *Ibid.*, p. 252.

9. Talcott Parsons, "The Normal American Family," in Marvin B. Sussman, ed., *Sourcebook of Marriage and the Family*, 3rd ed. (Boston: Houghton Mifflin, 1968), pp. 36-46. See also Marvin B. Sussman, "The Isolated Nuclear Family: Fact or Fiction?" in Sussman, ed., *Sourcebook of Marriage and the*

Family, 4th ed. (Boston: Houghton Mifflin, 1974), pp. 25-30.

10. Parsons, "The Normal American Family," p. 39.

11. W. F. Ogburn and M. F. Nimkoff, *Technology and the Changing Family* (Boston: Houghton Mifflin, 1955).

12. *Ibid.*, p. 290.

13. Ralph Linton, "The Natural History of the Family," *The Family: Its Function and Destiny*, ed. Ruth Nanda Anshen, pp. 30-52.

14. Richard R. Clayton, *The Family, Marriage and Social Change* (Lexington, Mass.: D.C. Heath, 1975), p. 68.

15. *Ibid.*, pp. 178-86.

16. *Ibid.*, pp. 170-8.

17. Gerald R. Leslie, *The Family in Social Context*, 4th ed. (New York: Oxford University Press, 1979), pp. 200-5.

18. Clayton, pp. 80-4, and Leslie, pp. 205-12.

19. Ogburn and Nimkoff state that "a surprisingly large number of changes in family living in the past century or two in the United States can be traced to three clusters of inventions and discoveries, those centering around steam and steel, contraceptives, and scientific discoveries affecting forms of religious beliefs. There are, however, ideological forces producing changes in the family that cannot be adequately traced to technological or scientific origins" (p. iii). *the Changing Family*, p. iii.

20. Clayton, p. 80.

21. Leslie, pp. 212-20.

22. Quoted in Clayton, p. 89.

23. *Ibid.*, p. 69.

24. *Ibid.*, p. 69.

25. *Ibid.*, p. 73.

26. Quoted in Clayton, p. 73.

27. J. Richard Udry, *The Social Context of Marriage* (Philadelphia: Lippincott, 1971), p. 15.

28. *Ibid.*, p. 15.

29. *Ibid.*, p. 16.

30. The above is based on the Prospectus of the Project, Revised Edition, January 1, 1977, p. 1. The following material is based on *Family Power Social Change Project, 1976-79: A Summary Analysis* prepared by Ross T. Bender, Research Associate (1979-80) to the Office of Family Education, World Council of Churches, Geneva, Switzerland. It is included in the Report of the Drafting Committee of the Oaxtepec meeting published in Geneva in 1980 under the title, *Report of Family Education World Assembly: Participation of Families in Social Change*.

Chapter 5

1. Jewett, *Man as Male and Female*, p. 24.

2. Rosemary Haughton, *The Mystery of Sexuality* (New York: Paulist Press, 1972), p. 9.

3. *Ibid.*, p. 32.

4. Udry, *The Social Context of Marriage*, p. 17.

5. Wilhelm Reich, *The Sexual Revolution*, trans. by Theodore P. Wolfe (New

York: Octagon Books, 1971), p. xv.

6. James B. Nelson, for example, states, "Sexuality, it is said, has been artificially repressed. We must throw off the social masks, reclaim our inner forces and feelings, and in this way be united with a cosmic vitality. . . . But, curiously, the members of this school do not seem to regard sexual expression and sexual love as truly personal" (*Embodiment*, p. 71).

7. Heini Arnold, *In the Image of God: Marriage and Chastity in Christian Life* (Rifton, N.Y.: Plough Publishing House, 1977).

8. *Ibid.*, pp. 61-2.

9. *Ibid.*, p. 118.

10. Brunner, *The Divine Imperative*, pp. 512-3.

11. Carl Rogers, *Freedom To Learn* (Columbus, Ohio: Charles E. Merrill Publishing Co., 1969), pp. 158-9.

12. Howe, *Man's Need and God's Action*, pp. 65-76.

13. Brunner, *The Divine Imperative*, p. 210.

14. *Ibid.*, p. 330.

15. *Ibid.*, p. 336-7.

16. *Ibid.*, p. 331.

17. Johannes Pederson, *Israel, Its Life and Culture* (London: Oxford University Press, 1946), I, 48-100.

18. *Ibid.*, pp. 48-9.

The Author

Ross Thomas Bender is currently professor of Christian education at the Associated Mennonite Biblical Seminaries, Elkhart, Indiana, where he has been a member of the faculty for twenty years. From 1964 to 1979 he served as dean of the faculty; during this time he led the faculties of Goshen Biblical Seminary and Mennonite Biblical Seminary (the member schools in the association) in a study of the theological and educational foundation of their curriculum. This was a major part of the process of bringing their programs together on a common campus.

Bender has been an educator for thirty years, first in the public schools of Oxford County, Ontario, Canada, later as principal of Rockway Mennonite High School, Kitchener, Ontario, and more recently as a seminary teacher and administrator. His interest in family studies, both as educator and therapist, have continued to grow alongside his other responsibilities. His doctoral dissertation at Yale University (1962) was on "The Role of the Contemporary Family in Christian Nurture: A Theological Interpretation." A decade later he was an NIMH postdoctoral fellow in the Division of Family Studies, Department of Psychiatry, School of Medicine, University of Pennsylvania, Philadelphia.

Since that time he has been a clinical member of the American Association for Marital and Family Therapy; currently he serves on the board of directors of its Indiana section. During his most recent sabbatical leave (1979-80) while preparing the present lectureship, "Christians in Families," he served part-time as research associate to the Office of Family Education of the World Council of Churches in Geneva, Switzerland.

Ross and Ruth Bender (a professional librarian as well as homemaker) are the parents of five children and the grandparents of a little boy who lives with his parents in southern Idaho. Four of their five children were born in Canada, where Ross and Ruth were raised. Their youngest daughter, the only American-born member of the family, entered college in September 1982. "We have pretty well completed the launching phase of the family life cycle and look forward to what the next stages hold in store for us," they said. "We enjoy being with our children and their spouses on those rare occasions when we can all get together. Our home in Goshen is a long way from Idaho and New York City, where our sons are presently living, but we all manage to stay in touch with each other."

The Benders are members of the College Mennonite Church in Goshen, Indiana, where he has served as a member of the board of elders. In the past, Ross has been an associate pastor (Waterloo, Ontario, and Lansdale, Pennsylvania) and has served on several churchwide commissions and boards. He is the present chairman of the Mennonite Church General Board and moderator of the Mennonite General Assembly which includes chairing its biennial session in August 1983, on the occasion of the 300th anniversary of the coming of the Mennonites to the New World in 1683.

The Conrad Grebel Lectures

The Conrad Grebel Lectureship was set up in 1950 to make possible an annual study by a Mennonite scholar of some topic of interest and value to the Mennonite Church and to other Christian people. It is administered by the Conrad Grebel Projects Committee appointed by and responsible to the Mennonite Board of Education. The committee appoints the lecturers, approves their subjects, counsels them during their studies, and arranges for the delivery of the lectures at one or more places.

Conrad Grebel was an influential leader in the sixteenth-century Swiss Anabaptist movement and is honored as one of the founders of the Mennonite Church.

The lectures are published by Herald Press, Scottdale, Pa. 15683, and Kitchener, Ont. N2G 4M5, as soon as feasible after the delivery of the lectures. The date of publication by Herald Press is indicated by parenthesis.

Lectures thus far delivered are as follows:

1952—*Foundations of Christian Education,*
      by Paul Mininger.
1953—*The Challenge of Christian Stewardship* (1955),
      by Milo Kauffman.
1954—*The Way of the Cross in Human Relations*
      (1958),
      by Guy F. Hershberger.
1955—*The Alpha and the Omega* (1955),
      by Paul Erb.
1956—*The Nurture and Evangelism of Children*
      (1959),
      by Gideon G. Yoder.
1957—*The Holy Spirit and Holy Life* (1959),
      by Chester K. Lehman.

1959—*The Church Apostolic* (1960),
 by J. D. Graber.
1960—*These Are My People* (1962),
 by Harold S. Bender.
1963—*Servant of God's Servants* (1964),
 by Paul M. Miller.
1964—*The Resurrected Life* (1965),
 by John R. Mumaw.
1965—*Creating Christian Personality* (1966),
 by A. Don Augsburger.
1966—*God's Word Written* (1966),
 by J. C. Wenger.
1967—*The Christian and Revolution* (1968),
 by Melvin Gingerich.
1968-1969—*The Discerning Community: Church Renewal,*
 by J. Lawrence Burkholder.
1970—*Woman Liberated* (1971),
 by Lois Gunden Clemens.
1971—*Christianity and Culture: An African Context,*
 by Donald R. Jacobs.
1973—*In Praise of Leisure* (1974),
 by Harold D. Lehman.
1977—*Integrity: Let Your Yea Be Yea* (1978),
 by J. Daniel Hess.
1979—*The Christian Entrepreneur* (1980),
 by Carl Kreider.
1980—*From Word to Life* (1982),
 by Perry Yoder.
1980—*Case Issues in Biblical Interpretation* (1983),
 by Willard M. Swartley.
1981—*Christians in Families* (1982),
 by Ross T. Bender.